KU-690-489

Counting the Days to Armageddon

The Jehovah's Witnesses and The Second Presence of Christ

Robert Crompton

UNIVERSITY OF WOLVERHAMPTON
LIBRARY

ACC No. 2095060

CONTROL
0227679393

DATE
-1 JUL 1997

SITE
WL

CLASS
289.
92
CRO

James Clarke & Co
Cambridge

James Clarke & Co
P.O. Box 60
Cambridge
CB1 2NT

British Library Cataloguing in Publication Data:
A catalogue record is available from the British Library.

ISBN 0 2276 7939 3

Copyright © Robert Crompton 1996

The rights of Robert Crompton to be identified as the
Author of this work have been asserted by him in accordance with the
Copyright Designs and Patents Act 1988.

All rights reserved. No part of this publication may be reproduced,
stored in a retrieval system or transmitted in any form or by any means,
electronic, mechanical, photocopying, recording or otherwise,
without the prior permission in writing of the Publisher.

Printed in Great Britain by Hillman Printers, (Frome) Ltd.

Contents

Acknowledgments

It is my pleasant duty to record my indebtedness to several people who have helped in various ways during the writing of this book, the original version of which was a thesis for the degree of MLitt in the University of Durham. I am particularly grateful to Dr Sheridan Gilley for his help and encouragement. The Darlington and Leeds Districts of the Methodist Church contributed to the costs of my research. Carl Hagensick, James Parkinson and Eric Williams provided valuable information concerning the various groups of Bible Students who seceded from the Watch Tower Society. Raymond Franz read and commented upon a late draft, and supplied me with information concerning the authorship of much of the Watch Tower Societies Literature. Mrs Hole of Newbold College library was most helpful in directing me to the relevant Adventist sources. And special thanks go to the Revd Norman Valley who was able to locate some of the less easily obtainable but very important early Watch Tower sources. David Bowker alerted me to the major doctrinal change which called for substantial revision of the final chapter. In various ways these people have steered me away from errors I might otherwise have made. Those which remain are, of course, my own responsibility.

Tables

Chapter One
Introduction

Jehovah's Witnesses are well known for their vigorous door-to-door evangelism but, despite the intensiveness of their activities, they are generally not well understood. There has been an almost universal tendency, arising, perhaps from the perception of them as a movement belonging to the religious fringes, to underestimate their numerical strength and potential influence. A common picture of Witness activity, for many outside the movement, is of a small handful of workers faithfully calling at all the homes in their territory, year after year. Such may have been the picture a generation ago when small groups of 'pioneers' were seeking to establish Witness congregations in new territories, or when Kingdom Halls were often advertised by no more than a placard in the window of a rented upper storey. In many towns and cities throughout the world the reality is now very different with large congregations in their own premises and newly built Kingdom Halls an increasingly common sight.

Exact comparisons between the size of the Witness community and that of any other religious group are, of course, extremely difficult because the Witnesses acknowledge no category of membership which corresponds with the idea of church membership as it is found in most denominations. Some of the relevant figures, however, are easily obtained. In the 1 January issue of *The Watchtower* each year the Society [1] publishes its annual service report which compiles statistics from more than 200 countries where the Witnesses are active. Two figures given for each country in this report are of particular interest: Memorial attendance and 'publishers'. These constitute the range within which the comparison with any other denomination must be found. In 1992 the totals (for 229 countries) under these headings were 11,431,171 and 4,472,787 respectively.

The higher figure represents the attendance at the Witnesses' most important annual meeting, the Memorial, which is a commemoration of Jesus' Last Supper. All Witnesses make a special effort to be present at this meeting and to encourage newly interested persons, those who have drifted away but remain on the fringes of the movement and sympathetic family members to be present also. As a result, attendance at the Memorial is almost always much higher than at any other event. In some countries it may be felt that this figure represents a fair comparison with the membership of another denomination. More likely, however, it will seem to overstate the numerical strength of the Witness community.

The lower figure, the number of publishers, though it represents a category not usually found in other religious groups, is well defined and very illuminating. Publishers are active Witness evangelists who each spend, on average, about ten hours every month in door to door canvassing in addition to attendance at meetings and personal study. The figure does not include any who may attend meetings, however frequently, but who do not engage in the movement's public ministry. It will almost certainly, therefore, understate the numerical strength of the Witness community. Somewhere between these two figures, then, Memorial attendance and publishers, the true comparison with membership in the mainstream denominations must lie.

The annual service report also shows[2] the total population of each country where Witnesses are active. From this is calculated a ratio dividing the total population by the number of publishers. Table 1 shows the seven largest countries (taken arbitrarily as countries with a population in excess of fifty million) where the proportion of active Witnesses is greater than one in five hundred.[2]

Although the above figures may reveal Witness communities much larger than many may have imagined, even at their greatest they represent only a small fraction of the total population. When the ratio is regarded as the average size of the theoretical territory of every active Witness publisher, however, the figures strongly indicate that in all the major countries of the world the Witnesses constitute armies of evangelists far greater than the mainstream denominations are able to muster.

Despite their intensive activity, however, the doctrinal basis of the movement is generally not well understood within the mainstream churches. A number of factors contribute to this situation. There is often a disinclination to study the movement's doctrines in its own literature, arising, perhaps, from a desire not to get involved or to give any support to the movement. But the secondary sources at present available are often quite unreliable in ways that the general reader can be in no position to detect. Many writers of popular works betray an inadequate understanding of their subject and, indeed, are often prone to errors arising from failure to undertake the most basic research. Berry, for example, writing in 1987, asserted that:

> the Jehovah's Witnesses believe that the writings of Russell and Rutherford take precedence over the Bible. *Studies in the Scriptures* and Russell's other books still remain the primary source of authority.[3]

In fact, Rutherford's books had ceased to be circulated more than 40 years earlier whilst Russell's had been discarded in 1927. Both writers had long since ceased to be regarded as in any way authoritative, a fact which would have been obvious to anyone having sufficient familiarity with the Watch Tower[4] movement to write informatively about it.

Some of the apparently more thoroughly researched literature is, likewise, prone to avoidable error. Martin and Klann, for example, seek to refute the Witnesses' contention that they are not followers of C. T. Russell by an analysis of the doctrinal continuity between Russell and the present day Watch Tower movement.[5] In doing so, they prove only what has never been denied. Had their chapter on the history of the movement addressed itself to the

Table 1. *Seven of the Largest Witness Communities*

Brazil
Population:	146,154,502
Publishers:	335,039
Ratio:	1:436
Memorial Attendance:	985,252

Britain
Population:	56,033,899
Publishers:	126,173
Ratio:	1:444
Memorial Attendance:	224,654

France
Population:	56,900,000
Publishers:	119,674
Ratio:	1:475
Memorial Attendance:	230,068

Germany
Population:	80,136,903
Publishers:	163,095
Ratio:	1:491
Memorial Attendance:	284,180

Italy
Population:	57,576,429
Publishers:	194,013
Ratio:	1:297
Memorial Attendance:	362,167

Mexico
Population:	84,662,130
Publishers:	354,023
Ratio:	1:239
Memorial Attendance:	1,283,203

United States of America
Population:	250,472,000
Publishers:	904,963
Ratio:	1:277
Memorial Attendance:	1,939,220

development of the doctrines of the second presence of Christ and the Kingdom of God, which have always been of central importance, the discontinuity would have become apparent. Instead, it concentrates almost exclusively on personal attacks upon Russell and Rutherford which provide no basis whatever for the doctrinal study which follows.

The preoccupation with personal attacks of so many writers calls in question the objectivity and validity of their studies, especially in view of the fact that much of the material is used somewhat less than honestly. For example, Martin and Klann refer to Rutherford's imprisonment in 1918 'for violation of the *Espionage Act*',[6] without mentioning that he was subsequently exonerated. Similarly, Kellett refers to Russell's divorce 'on the grounds of his immoral conduct with members of his sect',[7] when in fact the evidence that was brought against him on that particular charge was rejected by the court.

In addition to the difficulties already noted, impartial, objective theological study of the Watch Tower movement is further hindered by the fact that most, if not all, of the secondary material addresses complex aims. Such material falls into two categories. On the one hand, there is what has been written, usually from a conservative evangelical perspective, with the dual aims of exposing Watch Tower error and promoting sound evangelical doctrine. Whilst such writing may accomplish its own purposes adequately, from the point of view of the wider church community it has limitations. Those who do not subscribe to evangelical doctrine will find different and, perhaps, fewer areas of Watch Tower teaching with which to take issue. This wider constituency is less adequately served by the literature.

On the other hand, there is that body of material which has been written by former members of the movement. Literature in this category usually does not seek to promote any alternative Christian position (though there are, of course, exceptions) but often betrays a level of hostility towards the movement which must raise doubts about the authors' capacity to provide objective accounts.[8]

In recent years, however, some interesting and useful works have appeared which do not conform to the established categories. Deserving special mention are Carl Olof Jonsson's *The Gentile Times Reconsidered*, Raymond Franz's *Crisis of Conscience* and *In Search of Christian Freedom*, and M. James Penton's *Apocalypse Delayed*. Jonsson's book is an extremely useful study of a small but important part of the chronological approach to prophecy with which this book is concerned. It was first written when the author was still a Jehovah's Witness; at the time of writing, Jonsson had no intention of leaving the Watch Tower movement but was eventually forced out by his researches and by the Society's hostile reaction to his work. Franz, who was a member of the Watch Tower Society's supreme council, the Governing Body, before leaving and being disfellowshipped because of conscientious disagreements, has provided a wealth of information about the inner workings of the Society which had previously been unavailable. Penton, a lecturer in Religious Studies in the University of Lethbridge, Canada, and a former Jehovah's Witness of long standing, has provided in his book what is by far the best general description of the Watch Tower movement currently available.

Despite the enormous contribution made by these works, theological understanding of the Watch Tower movement still lags far behind sociological understanding.[9] It is my intention in this book to contribute to the foundations of a proper theological description of Watch Tower doctrine, and particularly the second coming of Christ, the Millennium and the Kingdom of God. There is good reason to begin this theological study with these topics. They are at the centre of the movement's most distinctive doctrinal area, and it is in relation to these topics that the question whether and in what form the movement may survive into the twenty-first century, is raised. More importantly but less obviously, study of Watch Tower ideas concerning the Millennium and related issues reveals that the movement developed within a tradition which it does not itself recognise.

My interest in this subject is a longstanding one. I was brought up as a Jehovah's Witness, my parents having taken an interest in the movement during the mid-1940s. During the early 1960s I served as a full-time minister or 'special pioneer' until I began to have some serious doubts about Watch Tower doctrine. So far as the present topic is concerned, my doubts at that stage centred on two areas. It seemed to me that the Society's application of its own method of interpretation of prophecy was not entirely consistent. In the interpretation of some references to periods of time, the Society's procedure is to apply the 'rule' that one day in prophecy represents one year in the fulfilment. This rule is followed for the interpretation of Nebuchadnezzar's vision in Daniel 4 of a tree which is cut down and restrained from growth for 'seven times,' and for the prophecy of the 'seventy weeks' of Daniel 9, passages which figure prominently in Watch Tower doctrine. However, it is not followed for the interpretation of certain periods which occupy an apparently secondary place in the overall system, namely, the 1,260 days, 1,290 days, and 1,335 days of Daniel 12 and the 2,300 days of Daniel 8. Feeling this to be unsatisfactory, I began to probe a little more deeply and discovered that Charles Taze Russell, the Society's first President, had expounded a system of interpretation of prophecy which was very different from present Watch Tower teaching. As a loyal Witness, I had always supposed that the development of doctrine had proceeded by the gradual addition of detail, together with minor corrections, to an underlying structure which remained unchanged. In fact, this was not at all the pattern which I discovered; rather, one system had apparently been replaced by another which was, in some significant respects, less detailed and exhibited less internal consistency.

At this stage my disagreement with the Society concentrated mainly upon the fact that, under Russell's leadership, they had made many quite specific predictions which had failed to be realised, and that Rutherford, seeking to put right what had gone wrong, had added a further set of failures to the list. However, I have since come to believe that such an emphasis is unhelpful because it tends to obscure the more interesting and important underlying issues. It is entirely natural, though, for the former Witness and the evangelical polemicist to direct their attention to failed predictions without seeking to understand the basis upon which those predictions were made. The Society has nothing but contempt for other individuals and groups which have been shown to be wrong in their predictions of future events. To expose the Society's own deficiencies in this regard seems to go directly to the heart of the most crucial issues. In fact, it does not do so.

The serious theologian usually has little inclination to become concerned with doctrinal systems such as that of the Watch Tower movement. Those systems may be seen as the descendants of an approach to Christian belief which has been left behind by advances in biblical scholarship, in theology and in science. In time they will wither away. Such a view may be encouraged by the observation that the precursors of these doctrinal systems are generally to be found within the Christian mainstream but, as scholarship advances, they are increasingly associated with the fringes of the Church. As in scientific circles belief in a geocentric universe, phlogiston and phrenology became increasingly difficult to maintain, so in Christian circles the belief systems now associated mainly with the sectarian fringe will eventually come to appear incredible even to those who would otherwise have been their natural adherents. Groups such as Jehovah's Witnesses, it may be supposed, will eventually go the same way as the followers of Joanna Southcott and the like.

Such a view is oversimplified. The Watch Tower movement deserves serious study, not as a fascinating but, in the end, insignificant aberration, nor simply as an example of what may go wrong when church members are less well informed about Christian doctrine and its foundations than is desirable. Rather, it deserves study as a movement which has been steadily increasing its size and potential influence during a time when, in some countries, the mainstream denominations have been in decline. I do not believe that the Watch Tower movement is likely to disappear from the religious scene in the foreseeable future, but it may well be that it will begin to face increasing difficulties and suffer some reversal in its fortunes as it moves into the twenty-first century and tries to accommodate the protracted delay of the Battle of Armageddon. Any setback for the Watch Tower movement, however, should give the mainstream denominations no cause for rejoicing, for it is unlikely that it will suffer any loss of influence. Indeed, if the limited defections from the movement which have occurred in recent years were to continue and to be accompanied by the breaking down, amongst some factions, of some of the present hostility towards other denominations, then the resulting possibility of even limited dialogue, which has before now simply not existed, could mean that a weakened Watch Tower movement would be in a position, paradoxically, to exert greater influence than has the hitherto apparently monolithic society.

Notes

1. The term 'Society' is used somewhat loosely to refer to the upper echelons of the movement's leadership structures. In this usage, which follows the practice within the movement, 'Society' is nearly, but not completely, synonymous with 'Watch Tower Bible and Tract Society'. This should not be confused with another usage which was common at one time among Jehovah's Witnesses, in which 'Society' was an abbreviation of 'New World Society' and referred to the whole movement. To avoid confusion, this latter usage is avoided.
2. *The Watchtower*, 1 January 1993, p. 12.
3. Harold J. Berry, *The Truth Twisters*, p. 54f.

4. Following the Society's convention (to which there are some minor exceptions), the form 'Watchtower' is reserved for the magazine of that title. In all other instances the form, 'Watch Tower,' is used.

5. W. Martin and N. Klann, *Jehovah of the Watchtower*, pp. 36ff.

6. *Ibid.*, p. 26

7. A. Kellett, *Isms and Ologies*, p. 55.

8. See, for example, William J. Schnell, *Thirty Years a Watch Tower Slave*.

9. James A. Beckford, *The Trumpet of Prophecy*, for example, is a useful sociological study of the movement.

Chapter Two
The Scriptural Starting Point

The group of doctrinal systems within which the Watch Tower movement belongs, rests heavily upon a characteristic approach to the books of Daniel and Revelation as well as certain significant passages from elsewhere in the Bible. At the heart of this approach is a literal interpretation of Revelation 20 which speaks of a period of one thousand years (the Millennium) during which Satan is to be bound and the saints, being resurrected, are to reign with Christ. Those who follow what is known as the historicist approach believe that the relevant apocalyptic and prophetic passages of Scripture have their fulfilment during the course of world history and that the due time for the inauguration of the Millennium is indicated therein. Before turning to a brief survey of the varieties of millennialist speculation, then, a look at the scriptural starting point is called for. It should be noted that what follows is not intended to be evenly representative of the whole biblical corpus relevant to the doctrines of the Kingdom of God and the second coming. It concentrates upon those parts of Scripture which have been in the forefront of the kind of millennialism with which this study is concerned and reflects, therefore, some of the biblical priorities of that tradition.

Daniel
Daniel is commonly held to belong to the literary genre known as apocalyptic. Such writing began as a product of late pre-Christian Judaism and is exemplified in a number of works which bear the name of an ancient character as author but which are generally supposed by modern scholars to be the product of a later writer. Of these only Daniel came to be included in the Old Testament canon. Characteristic of apocalyptic writing is a clear differentiation between the present age and the age to come. The secrets of the coming age, when it is to come and the blessings it will bring, and the course of history during the present age leading up to the great climax, are revealed to a chosen few. They in turn keep the secret, for such knowledge is not to be made generally known until all is about to be fulfilled (Daniel 12:9,10).

Though apocalyptic, like prophecy, looks forward to divinely determined events yet future, it should not be regarded straightforwardly as a natural development from prophecy. Indeed, von Rad argues that there is no continuity at all between apocalyptic and prophecy.[1] The view of history in apocalyptic, he argues, is so fundamentally different from that of the prophets, that the two are incompatible and the one cannot be said to derive from the latter. The prophetic message is inextricably linked with Israel's history and traditions. The nation is already the beneficiary of God's saving acts and this is the guarantee that it will continue to be so. Such a view, however, is absent from apocalyptic. Here the saving act of God is seen purely as a future event. The course of history – world history, not only Israel's history – is predetermined and the great saving act is the culmination at which it eventually arrives.

This difference in the view of history is reflected in the conditional nature of some prophecy. For example:

If at any time I announce that a nation or kingdom is to be uprooted, torn down and destroyed, and if that nation I warned repents of its evil, then I will relent and not inflict on it the disaster I had planned. (Jeremiah 18:7,8) [2]

In the apocalyptic visions, on the other hand, the future is all of a piece with the past and the course of history cannot be changed.

Not only is Daniel quite distinct from the prophets, it is, so von Rad argues, distinct from much else of significance in Israel's traditions.

In fact, the traditions connected with the patriarchs, Exodus, or Zion all seem to lie outside Daniel's mental world. (Only in the prayer in Dan. ix.7ff. is there reference to Moses and to the Exodus.) [3]

This seems to me to overstate the case for it makes too much of the absence of explicit references to earlier traditions and ignores some possible implicit references. Indeed, the figure of Daniel does appear to have a close link with earlier tradition, for he is remarkably similar to Joseph (Genesis 39-41). Both are righteous men living in exile; both are noted for their God-given superior wisdom; both have the ability to interpret dreams; and both are entrusted with responsibility for affairs of state.

Nevertheless, the fact remains that Daniel is distinctive within the Old Testament canon. This raises the question of its relationship with other literary forms. Davies has argued that the designation of Daniel as apocalyptic is unhelpful, for it has led to chapters 7-12, the apocalyptic chapters, being treated separately from chapters 1-6, the narrative chapters. [4] The apocalyptic material has been studied within the context of other such literature external to the canon, rather than within its proper context which is the narrative of the first half of the book. The assumption that Daniel is to be ranked with apocalyptic should not be accepted uncritically, for although it has been argued that because it was included amongst the literature which came to regarded as canonical, it thus became a model for other apocalypses to follow and to develop, the reverse could plausibly be argued. The fact that Daniel was included in the canon of the Old Testament may indicate that it was, from the outset, recognised to have stronger affinities with the prophets than with apocalyptic.

Although the book falls into two clearly identifiable parts, narrative and visions, it forms a literary unity and the visions presuppose the narrative. They take up and develop themes which found their first expression in the first half of the book. The unity of the book, despite the distinctiveness of its two major sections, strongly suggests that the narrative passages represent a reworking of earlier material by the same author who supplied the apocalyptic passages. Thus Lacocque concludes:

> In the second half of the second century B.C.E., the redactor and veritable author of Daniel availed himself of the tales belonging to a popular cycle about Daniel.[5]

The unity of Daniel is most apparent in the similarity between the story of Nebuchadnezzar's dream of an image in chapter 2 and the vision of the four beasts in chapter 7. The same sequence of world history is described in each. More fundamentally, in both narrative and visions the course of history is seen as the outworking of divine providence. In each case the wise and righteous hero is privy to the divine secrets. And in each case the eventual outcome is the same: the triumph of the Kingdom of God over human history.

Two important points arise from this all-too-sketchy view of Daniel. The first is that the course of human history and its culmination in the final triumph of good over evil is indeed the central theme of apocalyptic in general and Daniel in particular. It follows that the historicist millennialist approach is in the apocalyptic tradition or, at least, is a natural development from that tradition and should not, therefore, be regarded, despite popular opinion, as being *fundamentally* mistaken. Particular millennialist interpretations may well be mistaken, but they are generally in the spirit of apocalyptic.

The second, related, point concerns the distinction between apocalyptic and prophecy. It is a distinction which historicism does not normally make but this should not be regarded as an omission, for, as was noted above, whether the distinction is to be made and, if so, how it is to be applied, are arguable. Indeed, when trying to understand a doctrinal system, it is desirable, so far as possible, to work with the same prior assumptions as those upon which the beliefs in question are based. Otherwise there will be a risk of arguing at cross purposes. In the case of the distinction between apocalyptic and the rest of Scripture, if that distinction is made too rigidly, it will, in effect, assign to a minor category that literature which the millennialist treats as of central importance. Our view of Scripture and its interpretation is often likely to be dominated by our view of those scriptural genres which we consider to be central. It is important, therefore, to make a special effort to keep in mind the fact that the millennialist regards apocalyptic as central, as prophecy *par excellence*, and to avoid assuming too readily that this is mistaken.

The New Testament

One does not have to read far in the New Testament before coming upon evidence that the first Christians expected Jesus to return in order to complete the work he had begun before his crucifixion.

> So when they met together they asked him, 'Lord are you at this time going to restore the kingdom to Israel?' He said to them, 'It is not for you to know the times or dates the Father has set by his own authority.' (Acts 1:6,7)

It is possible to trace the development of this belief through the New Testament, from the expectation of an imminent return, to the resigned acknowledgement that there may be a long time to wait.

> In the last days scoffers will come, scoffing and following their own

evil desires. They will say, 'Where is this coming he promised?' ...
But do not forget this one thing, dear friends: With the Lord a day is
like a thousand years, and a thousand years are like a day. The Lord is
not slow in keeping his promise, as some understand slowness. He is
patient with you, not wanting anyone to perish, but everyone to come
to repentance. But the day of the Lord will come like a thief. The
heavens will disappear with a roar; the elements will be destroyed by
fire, and the earth and everything in it will be laid bare. (2 Peter 3:3-
10)

The New Testament doctrine of the return of Christ is firmly rooted in the
synoptic gospels, in particular in Jesus' discourse in Matthew 24 (and Mark
13 and Luke 21). There are presented various signs which, Jesus said, would
mark the time of his coming and the end of the age. It has long been recognised
that certain motifs found in this discourse are drawn from Daniel.

One who causes desolation will place abominations on a wing of the
temple until the end that is decreed is poured upon him. (Daniel 9:27)

This is echoed in Jesus' words:

When you see standing in the holy place the abomination that causes
desolation, spoken of through the prophet Daniel – let the reader
understand – then let those who are in Judea flee to the mountains.
(Matthew 24:15,16)

The original reference is to the desecration of the temple by Antiochus
Epiphanes, but the appearance of the motif in Jesus' discourse is seen by
many, millennialists especially, as good reason to place the major fulfilment
of Daniel's prophecies in the future and not in the second century B.C.

The figure of the Son of Man may, likewise, be drawn from Daniel.

There before me was one like a son of man, coming with the clouds of
heaven. (Daniel 7:13)

They will see the Son of Man coming on the clouds of the sky, with
power and great glory. (Matthew 24:30)

Again, the quotation by Jesus is, for the millennialist, *prima facie* confirmation
that Daniel is of central importance to an understanding God's purposes.

Another motif which is recurrent throughout the synoptics and which may
also reflect what is found in Daniel is the Kingdom of God. That Daniel is,
indeed, the background from which Jesus' teaching about the Kingdom is
drawn, has been argued persuasively by Wenham.[6] If that is correct, then
millennialist preoccupations are not simply to be dismissed as eccentric.

In the time of those kings, the God of heaven will set up a kingdom
that will never be destroyed. (Daniel 2:44)

The kingdom to which Daniel refers, so millennialist belief generally has it,
is the same kingdom for which Christians pray in the Lord's Prayer and it will
be established during the coming Millennium.

It is in the book of Revelation, however, that the New Testament most
obviously provides a literary genre similar to that exemplified by the second
half of Daniel. Unlike many of the events portrayed in the apocalyptic chapters
of Daniel, however, the events described in Revelation are difficult to identify.
The application of Daniel to the course of world history until the time of
Antiochus Epiphanes (d. 163 BC) has widespread agreement. Those passages
which have been considered at any time to have been fulfilled in a later age

have also received widespread assent within the millennialist tradition. But those passages, on the other hand, which have seemed to predict events yet future have received many different interpretations. Revelation, unfortunately, is more like the latter than the former and, for that reason, has often been treated warily and regarded by many as the happy hunting-ground of the would-be prophet.

Despite this obvious difficulty, the background of much of Revelation's imagery can be traced or, at least, suggested. Indeed, that background is frequently alluded to in the text. So, for example, the woman riding the seven-headed, ten-horned beast of chapter 17 is identified with Babylon. What is symbolised by the woman, then, has important characteristics in common with ancient Babylon. It is not difficult to make the connection with Rome which, like Babylon, was a major centre of pagan religion and the oppressor of the people of God. The fall of Babylon prepares the way for the coming of what is to supplant it. Chapter 21 speaks of a new heaven and a new earth and describes the descent of the Holy City, or New Jerusalem. What is meant appears to be the inauguration, at the climax of history, of the Kingdom of God.

This much may be fairly certain, but it is the barest of outlines. That Revelation purports to supply the details of events leading up to the inauguration of the millennial kingdom is also fairly clear. Whether it may be possible to have confidence in any attempts to unravel Revelation's intricate symbolism, however, and learn what those details might be, is an entirely different matter. The millennialist is convinced that confidence in this area is justified.

Notes

1. Gerhard von Rad, *Old Testament Theology*, Vol 2, pp. 301ff.
2. All scripture quotations in this chapter are from the New International Version.
3. von Rad, *op. cit.*, p. 309.
4. P. R. Davies, 'Eschatology in the Book of Daniel', in *Journal for the Study of the Old Testament*, Vol. 17, 1980, pp. 33-53.
5. André Lacocque, *The Book of Daniel*, p. 10.
6. David Wenham, 'The Kingdom of God and Daniel', in *The Expository Times*, Vol 98, No. 5, February 1987, pp.132-134.

Chapter Three
The Historicist Millennialist Tradition

Implicit in much polemic directed against Jehovah's Witnesses is the assumption that their doctrines are incompatible with anything which may legitimately be described as Christian. For example, Martin and Klann declare that,

> They are deluded believers in the theology of one man, Charles Taze Russell, who was proven to be neither a Christian nor a qualified Bible student. [1]

Such an attitude makes it difficult to appreciate the relation of the Watch Tower movement to the tradition within which it arose. Moreover, it is a psychologically unsound approach, even for the purposes of the polemicist, because it unwittingly concedes a major claim made by the Watch Tower movement: namely, that they are entirely distinct from all other religious groups. In what follows, therefore, I shall avoid addressing the question, Christian or not Christian? As this enquiry proceeds, however, it will become evident how far the movement has distanced itself from the Protestant mainstream.

The Watch Tower doctrine of the Millennium belongs within a tradition of interpretation of Scripture which has been subject to trial and error since the first century AD, when some Jewish rabbis sought to identify the due time for the appearance of Messiah by their interpretation of the prophecy of the seventy weeks of Daniel 9:24-27.[2] This approach to prophetic interpretation, which is based upon the principle that one day in prophecy represents one year in the fulfilment, was probably introduced into Christian exposition by the Cistercian Joachim of Flora (*circa* AD 1130-1202) who appears to have been the first Christian interpreter to apply the year-for-a-day rule to those time periods of Daniel and Revelation which have since exercised the minds of millennialists. The rule is not entirely arbitrary but does derive from Scripture, in particular from Ezekiel 4 where, in the prophet's enactment of the siege of Jerusalem, one day is stated to represent one year of the people's sin, and from Numbers 14 where the Israelites' forty years of wandering in the desert, following the Exodus, are described as a punishment for their failure to enter Canaan and are said to be determined by the forty days that the spies were surveying the land.

Following Joachim, many interpreters sought to identify the periods to which the prophecies referred. From the time of the Reformation the view became current in Protestant circles that the Roman Catholic Church was Antichrist and that the 'time, times and half a time' (that is, three and a half years) of Daniel 12:7 are identical to the 1,260 days of Revelation 11:2,3 and refer to the duration of Rome's power to oppress the true Church. The expiry of the 1,260 years thus indicated, then, would mark the demise of the papacy and the inauguration of the Millennium, the thousand year reign of Christ in which good at last triumphs over evil. For those who felt able to identify the period's beginning, it was a relatively easy matter to calculate the due time for its end and the climax of history. Jonsson lists thirty-six published attempts to identify the 1,260 years, from that of Joachim in the twelfth century to that of John Aquila Brown in the early nineteenth century. [3]

Though it may be supposed that persistent trial and error over such a long period would eventually lead to the abandonment of the year-for-a-day principle, a number of apparent successes seemed to confirm the validity of the principle. The exposition of the seventy weeks, as will become apparent in due course, seemed to provide outstanding validation of the approach, to the satisfaction of its Christian adherents if not to the satisfaction of its Jewish originators. And Robert Fleming, in his book *The Rise and Fall of the Papacy*, which was published in 1701, had this to say about events to be expected at the close of the eighteenth century:

> We may justly suppose that the French monarchy, after it has scorched others, will itself consume by doing so – its fire, and that which is the fuel which maintains it, wasting insensibly, till it be exhausted at last towards the end of this century. I cannot but hope that some new mortification of the chief supporters of the Antichrist will then happen; and perhaps the French monarchy may begin to be considerably humbled about that time. [4]

When events towards the end of the century, during the French Revolution, appeared to confirm Fleming's predictions, his book was reprinted both in England and in the United States of America where it enjoyed considerable acclaim. It was at this time particularly that interest in prophetic speculation began to gather momentum in Britain.

> The French Revolution was directly responsible for the revival of prophetic concern. To live through the decade of the 1790s in itself constituted an experience of apocalypticism for many of the British. [5]

It should be noted that at this stage the study of millennialism is not concerned exclusively with theological eccentrics or the Christian fringe. These views continued to be found well within the Protestant mainstream during the early nineteenth century.[6] In Britain millennialist speculation began to attract a following amongst some evangelicals from about the 1820s onwards. Of particular note, in the context of the present study, was James Hatley Frere who, in 1815, had published *A Combined View of the Prophecies of Daniel, Esdras, and St. John*, in which he expressed the belief that the second coming would be not a literal event but a spiritual one and would take place in 1822-3. Others expected a literal, personal appearance of Christ but it was a similar view to that of Frere that was to become an important part of Russell's belief system later in the century. Lewis Way, of the London Society for Promoting Christianity among the Jews, began to draw attention to the connection between the prophecies of the restoration of the Jewish people and the second coming. Amongst those who were influenced by Way's views was Henry Drummond who organised a series of prophetic conferences at Albury Park, Surrey between 1826 and 1830. By 1829 the Albury conferences had reached a series of conclusions which defined what was to amount to a prevailing orthodoxy in millennialist circles for a time.

1. This 'dispensation' or age will not end 'insensibly' but cataclysmically in judgment and destruction of the church in the same manner in which the Jewish dispensation ended.
2. The Jews will be restored to Palestine during the time of judgment.
3. The judgment to come will fall principally upon Christendom.
4. When the judgment is past, the millennium will begin.
5. The second advent of Christ will occur before the millennium.
6. The 1260 years of Daniel 7 and Revelation 13 ought to be measured from the reign of Justinian to the French Revolution. The vials of wrath (Revelation 16) are now being poured out and the second advent is imminent.[7]

At the same time that interest in millennialism was gaining ground in Britain, its popularity was also increasing in the United States of America. Sandeen has suggested that although it may not be possible to trace all the lines of influence, links between the two countries were strong and it may be assumed that the parallel development of millennialist thinking was not coincidental.[8]

It was during this period, however, that historicist millennialism came increasingly to be associated with those who gathered around themselves groups of adherents who were to become the precursors of the movements with which the views are now associated. Even so, the groups which began to emerge in the United States of America during the nineteenth century did not at first bear all the characteristics of today's sect. It is perhaps more illuminating to compare them with the house church movement of recent years – a loosely organised body grouped, not around any organisational structure, but around a set of ideas. Those who followed Miller, for example, were to be found at first in most Protestant denominations and did not begin to separate themselves and develop their own ecclesiology until a comparatively late stage when prompted to do so by ridicule from within the churches.

Nor was Charles Taze Russell straightforwardly the founder of a sect as he is frequently styled; rather he established a publishing concern. What was later to develop into the Watch Tower movement had its origins prior to his involvement and was at first only loosely organised. As it gathered momentum, and Russell emerged as sole leader, he exerted more and more influence over the local congregations through his control of the army of colporteurs distributing his literature, but the congregations remained autonomous. Further, although separation from the mainstream was well advanced by this stage, it was by no means complete and the movement continued to enjoy much support from people who remained within their denominations.[9] It was not until the presidency of Russell's successor that the congregations were at last brought under the complete control of the Society. The secessionist groups which emerged during this period, however, have retained much of the character of early movement.

Early Adventism in the United States

The nineteenth century saw the migration of historicist millennialist beliefs from the Protestant mainstream to the sectarian fringe in the United States. If one factor in this movement had been the diminishing credibility of this variety of millennialism amongst writers and preachers most directly influenced by contemporary scholarship, another factor was, perhaps, the general religious climate in the United States. Damsteegt, writing from a Seventh-day Adventist perspective, has argued that constitutionally guaranteed religious freedom led to a pluralism in the United States which was not found to the same extent elsewhere, and that this in turn resulted in a weakening of the major denominations in comparison with their European counterparts.[10] The result was a situation in which new religious movements could more easily be formed, and gifted amateur theologians could exert considerable influence.

American society was, perhaps, particularly receptive to millennialist ideas. Among the early Puritan settlers, the view had been prevalent that they were creating God's new Israel. This attitude was reflected later when many came to regard the American Revolution in religious terms, and sermons were frequently preached linking the newly formed republic with coming millennial glory.[11] At this stage the main emphasis was upon postmillennialism, the belief that gradual improvement of human society would usher in the Millennium, which would be followed by the second coming of Christ.

Premillennialism, on the other hand, which had become the orthodoxy of the Albury conferences in Britain, is the belief that the second coming of Christ will precede and inaugurate the Millennium. During the first half of the nineteenth century, premillennialism in the United States is associated mainly, though by no means exclusively, with William Miller (1782-1849).[12] As a young man Miller forsook his religious upbringing and became a deist. After his army service during the War of Independence, he embarked upon a search for deeper significance to life and, following an experience of conversion to Christianity, joined the Baptist Church. He then began a period of intensive Bible study in order to be able to justify his new faith to his deist friends, and it was this study which led him to his millennialist convictions. He became convinced that the second advent was to be premillennial and, indeed, within his own lifetime.

Miller began his career as a preacher and writer in 1831 when popular interest in the imminence of the second coming of Christ was already strong within the Protestant churches. He first set out his own distinctive ideas in a series of articles which he published in a Baptist weekly, the *Vermont Telegraph*, and which were reprinted in 1833 in the form of a booklet under the title *Evidences from Scripture and History of the Second Coming of Christ, about the Year 1843*. His views gained a wide following of people who, although they were labelled 'Millerites,' remained within their own churches for some years.

Miller's approach to the interpretation of Scripture was, generally speaking, well within the Protestant tradition, being based upon the principles of *sola scriptura*, the unity and the self-authentication of Scripture. He identified seven rules of interpretation which are exemplified in his exposition of the prophecies concerning the second coming and the Millennium. First, the canon of Scripture provides the context for its interpretation. Second, every word and sentence is important and must be given due consideration. Third, Scripture is its own expositor and, therefore, gives clear indications in several cases of how a passage is to be expounded. Fourth, one portion of Scripture may need to be interpreted by analogy with another. Fifth, there exist in Scripture prophetic parallels which are complementary to each other and require integration in order to reveal their meaning. Sixth, the literal sense of a passage must be given preference so long as it makes good sense. Seventh, some recurrent motifs have symbolic meaning. [13]

The meaning of symbols is supplied on the basis of analogy of Scripture. So, for example, the use of one day to represent one year is established in Ezekiel's enactment of the siege of Jerusalem (Ezekiel 4:6) and in the punishment of the Israelites for their faint-heartedness on the borders of Canaan (Numbers 14:34). By analogy, this principle may be extended in order to interpret the prophecies of Daniel and Revelation. Other symbols are assigned their meaning by a similar process. Having determined the meaning of the symbols, the next step was to locate a historical event which would literally fulfil every word of the passage under consideration, and which would harmonise with similarly interpreted passages elsewhere.

Miller's approach to the interpretation of the prophetic material also made use of typology. A 'type' is to be distinguished from a prophecy; it is an actual historical situation which prefigures a corresponding situation, the 'antitype'. Prophecy and typology may be combined so that a prophecy is fulfilled in miniature in one event (the 'type') but has its complete or major fulfilment in another (the 'antitype'). For example, the various prophecies relating to the Babylonian exile and the subsequent return and the rebuilding of Jerusalem, have only a partial fulfilment in those events. Their major fulfilment is seen in the captivity of the Church, the destruction of 'mystical' Babylon and the glorification of the saints in New Jerusalem.

The Time of the End

> But thou, O Daniel, shut up the words, and seal the book, even to the time of the end: many shall run to and fro, and knowledge shall be increased. . . . And he said, Go thy way, Daniel: for the words are closed up and sealed till the time of the end. (Daniel 12:4,9)[14]

Some of Miller's followers believed that the 'time of the end' was a point, marked by a single event; others believed that a period was represented. Miller himself thought that it referred to the end of the power of the pope over the Church, and the end of papal influence over civil governments. This occurred on 15 February 1798, during the French Revolution, when the French general, Berthier, entered Rome without resistance, deposed the pope, abolished papal government and erected the Republic of Italy.[15]

Others, whilst retaining the key event, expanded the idea of the 'time of the end'. Principal amongst these was Josiah Litch, who believed that 1798 saw the unsealing of Daniel so that the meaning of its prophecies could at last be discovered. In particular, it was then that the period meant by 'a time, times, and an half' (Daniel 12:7) became clear. For Litch, then, the 'time of the end' was not a single event but the period extending from 1798 until the second coming.

1,260 Days

How long shall it be to the end of these wonders?. . . It shall be for a time, times and an half; and when he shall have accomplished to scatter the power of the holy people, all these things shall be finished.(Daniel 12:6,7)

The interpretation of the 1,260 days provides an example of bringing together parallel prophecies from different parts of Scripture in order to understand an integrated whole. It has already been noted above that the symbolic meaning of days draws upon the analogy with Ezekiel 4:6 and Numbers 14:34. To identify the exact reference of the period which can thus be computed, there are drawn together prophecies from Daniel 2 and 7 and from Revelation 11 and 12.

In Daniel 2 there is described a statue seen by Nebuchadnezzar in a dream. It comprises a head made of gold, breast and arms of silver, belly and thighs of brass and legs of iron with feet partly of iron and partly of clay. A partial interpretation is given in verses 36-45, in which the golden head is said to represent Babylon and the other components its successor empires. Finally:

In the days of these kings shall the God of heaven set up a kingdom,
which shall never be destroyed. (Daniel 2:44)

Daniel 7 tells of a dream of four beasts which, likewise, represent a succession of empires until:

The judgement shall sit, and they shall take away his dominion, to consume and to destroy it unto the end. And the kingdom and dominion, and the greatness of the kingdom under the whole heaven, shall be given to the people of the saints of the most High, whose kingdom is an everlasting kingdom. (Daniel 7:26,27)

It is a fairly simple matter to put the main details of these two visions together and to identify the world empires which may be represented. In doing so, Miller followed a long-established tradition.

The interest of the millennialist is directed towards the fourth empire, represented in chapter 2 by the legs of iron and the feet of iron and clay, and in chapter 7 by the unnamed beast with ten horns. The empire is Rome and the toes and horns are the ten kingdoms into which the Roman empire was divided about AD 476, but there is no universal agreement concerning the identity of these ten kingdoms. The little horn which came up amongst the other ten is of particular interest to Miller. He believed that it represented the oppressive power of papal Rome the extent of whose reign is indicated thus:

And he shall speak great words against the most High, and shall wear out the saints of the most High, and think to change times and laws: and they shall be given into his hand until a time and times and the dividing of time. (Daniel 7:25)

The same period of oppression is mentioned in Revelation:

I will give power unto my two witnesses, and they shall prophesy a thousand two hundred and threescore days, clothed in sackcloth. (Revelation 11:3)

And to the woman were given two wings of a great eagle, that she might fly into the wilderness, into her place, where she is nourished for a time, and times, and half a time, from the face of the serpent. (Revelation 12:14)

The woman represents the Church, the two witnesses represent the Bible, the Old and New Testaments, and the prophecies echo the same wearing out of the saints spoken of in Daniel. In each case, the period is three-and-a-half times or 1,260 days which, on the basis that one day stands for one year, indicates the extent of papal power.

Whilst it should be clear at this stage that Miller follows in a long-established tradition of interpretation, it is important to note that the logical sequence of his thought is significantly different from that of his eighteenth-century predecessors. Many of those millennialists, convinced that 1,260 years was to be the extent of papal power, sought to establish the point at which that power began and hence projected its end. Miller, with the advantage of recent history, and evidently following the developments in millennialist thinking during the early nineteenth century, was able first to identify an event, Berthier's entry into Rome in 1798, which appeared to fulfil this interpretation of the prophecies, and then to calculate from there the point at which the 1,260 years might be deemed to have begun. That it was possible, in this manner, to locate an event which appeared to be a reasonable starting point for the 1,260 years – Justinian's recognition in AD 538 of the pope as universal bishop – was strong confirmation of his thinking but was not at all essential. Indeed, it is entirely in keeping with the belief that the prophecies of Daniel are incapable of being fully understood until the 'time of the end', that there should be vagueness and uncertainty surrounding the starting point until the end point can be confirmed.

Cleansing the Sanctuary

How long shall be the vision concerning the daily sacrifice, and the transgression of desolation, to give both the sanctuary and the host to be trodden underfoot? And he said unto me, Unto two thousand and three hundred days; then shall the sanctuary be cleansed. (Daniel 8:13,14)

With the 1,260 days fulfilled and satisfactorily explained, the 2,300 days of Daniel 8:14 began to engage the attention of millennialists during the first half of the nineteenth century. [16] The year-for-a-day principle had resulted in two major interpretations of the little horn (Daniel 7:8), namely, pagan and papal Rome and Islam. These two views led naturally to two corresponding views of the cleansing of the sanctuary. Those who believed that the little horn represented Islam saw the cleansing of the sanctuary in terms of the liberation of Palestine and Jerusalem from the Muslims, the dissolution of Islam and the fall of Turkey; those who identified Rome with the little horn looked for some form of cleansing of the Church and restoration of true worship, together with the destruction of the papal Antichrist. In either case, the cleansing of the sanctuary would herald the start of the Millennium, the establishment of the Kingdom, the Day of Judgement and the return of Christ.

Miller believed that the sanctuary had seven possible references, of which just two made sense of the prophecy. Jesus Christ and heaven do not stand in any need of cleansing; the ancient kingdom of Judah, the temple and its holy of holies, having ceased to exist can no longer be cleansed. This left the earth and the saints; both would make sense of the prophecy and Miller believed that both would, in their different ways, be cleansed at the coming of Christ.

The beginning of the 2,300 days is identified by comparison with the prophecy of the seventy weeks in Daniel 9 which

> are determined upon thy people and upon thy holy city, to finish the transgression, and to make an end of sins, and to make reconciliation for iniquity, and to bring in everlasting righteousness, and to seal up the vision and prophecy, and to anoint the most Holy. (Daniel 9:24)

The two periods apparently share a theme in common: 'to finish the transgression' (seventy weeks) and 'how long shall be the vision concerning . . . the transgression?' (2,300 days). For that reason, Miller believed that the two shared a common starting point, namely 'the going forth of the commandment to restore and to build Jerusalem' (Daniel 9:25). That the command to rebuild Jerusalem was given in 457 BC was confirmed by the prophecy's fulfilment 490 years later in AD 33 with the crucifixion of Jesus. The 2,300 years, then, begin at the same time and extend to AD 1843.

The Year of the Resurrection

> And from the time that the daily sacrifice shall be taken away, and the abomination that maketh desolate set up, there shall be a thousand two hundred and ninety days. Blessed is he that waiteth, and cometh to the thousand three hundred and five and thirty days. (Daniel 12:11,12)

Miller interpreted Daniel 12:11,12 by comparing it with 2 Thessalonians 2:7 where a similar idea seems to be echoed:

> For the mystery of iniquity doth already work: he who now letteth will let, until he be taken out of the way.

The 'mystery of iniquity' and the 'abomination that maketh desolate' both refer to papal Rome; the hindering power, 'he who letteth', is paganism. So, by analogy, the daily sacrifice signified pagan religion which eventually gave way to the papacy. Since it is already known that the end of the papal power came with the end of the 1,260 days in 1798, it may be inferred that the 1,290 days end in 1798 also. Consequently, counting back 1,290 years, AD 508 is identified as the year when Roman paganism effectively ceased to exist.

This provides the starting point for the 1,335 days which therefore extend to AD 1843. Comparing Daniel 12:12, '*blessed* is he that waiteth', with Revelation 20:6, '*blessed* and holy is he that hath part in the first resurrection,' Miller inferred that the end of the 1,335 days was the due time for the first resurrection to take place.

Further Indications

Miller found other indications in scripture giving confirmation of the year AD 1843. In his prophecy of the second coming, Jesus said:

> And they shall fall by the edge of the sword, and shall be led away captive into all nations: and Jerusalem shall be trodden down of the Gentiles, until the times of the Gentiles be fulfilled. (Luke 21:24)

This, he believed, reiterates a much earlier prophecy:

> I will chastise you seven times for your sins. . . . And I will scatter you among the heathen, and will draw out a sword after you: and your

land shall be desolate, and your cities waste. (Leviticus 26:28,33)
The 'times of the Gentiles' refers to the period of this chastisement and its length is indicated by the expression 'seven times'. A time is a year of 360 days, so, applying the year-for-a-day principle, seven times indicates a period of 2,520 years. It began to count in 677 BC when Israelite people were first taken into captivity, that is, when first the prophetic warning in Leviticus 26 began to be fulfilled, and ends in AD 1843.

The ancient Jewish Jubilee year was seen as a prophetic type of the millennial age to come, and the due time for the Millennium to begin was calculated by analogy with the timing of that festival. As the Jubilee was the fiftieth year, so the Millennium takes the place of a fiftieth fifty-year period. That is, the Millennium, the antitypical Jubilee, is due to begin 2,450 years from the time when the typical Jubilee ceased to be observed. This occurred in 607 BC with the destruction of Jerusalem and the Babylonian exile. Once again, the beginning of the Millennium is confirmed as AD 1843

Finally, as 'one day is with the Lord as a thousand years' (2 Peter 3:8), so the seventh thousand years may be regarded as a sort of sabbath. Since the year AD 1843 is six thousand years after the creation, it marks the beginning of the great sabbath, the Millennium.

The Parable of the Ten Virgins
When the due time for the fulfilment of the prophecies arrived, inevitably there was found to be cause for revision. First, it was realised that the relevant calendar for such calculations would be the Jewish calendar, not the Gregorian and, on this basis, the year in question would be shifted to the period between March 1843 and March 1844. Secondly, it was then realised that since year numbers are ordinals, it was a mistake to compute periods from BC to AD by simply adding the year numbers together. That is, there is no zero year; consequently 2,300 years forward from 457 BC comes to AD 1844. [17]

These minor adjustments in the calculations, together with a diversity of individual opinion among Adventists regarding specific dates, were, perhaps, factors in helping to keep faith and expectancy alive despite the failure of hopes in 1844. But if the movement was to survive, a satisfactory explanation for the continued delay of the coming of Christ would have to be found. Such an explanation was provided by the parable of the wise and foolish virgins (Matthew 25:1-13), the details of which were readily transferable to the situation following the disappointed Adventist hopes: 'the bridegroom tarried'. Those who were unprepared for the delay lost their chance of admittance to the marriage feast, but the wise and faithful remained alert.

The period following 1844, then, came to be seen as a time of sifting. Some abandoned their Adventist beliefs, some treated the failure as a failure in calculation, and others took the view that the calculations were correct but the nature of what was to happen had been misunderstood.

The Rise of Seventh-day Adventism
It was a small minority amongst Miller's following who formed the group which was to become the Seventh-day Adventist Church. They maintained that Miller's interpretation of the prophecies had been correct in all essentials, but that he had been mistaken in the details. Where Miller had expected 1843

to see the cleansing of the earthly sanctuaries, that is, the earth itself and the saints, the Seventh-day Adventists believed that it was the heavenly sanctuary that was involved and that the prophecy had, indeed, been fulfilled in 1843 as calculated. There began at that time the 'investigative judgement' whereby the justice of God's judgement is made plain and the names of the righteous are retained in the book of life whilst the appropriate punishment for the wicked is determined. The second coming would occur at the completion of the judgement but the date of that is not indicated in Scripture.[18]

This reinterpretation of Miller's ideas seems to represent a source of considerable potential resilience for the Seventh-day Adventists. It makes it possible to retain the essential core of his system and so to remain a distinctively millennialist movement; but at the same time it allows the letting-go of an approach to millennialism which must stand in constant need of confirmation or revision and which, for that reason, will always be potentially disillusioning.

It should not pass unnoticed that it had not been the intention of the early Adventists to form themselves into a separate religious organisation. They were, at first, content to remain within their old denominations. But they began to develop an ecclesiology of their own following the disappointment of 1843 and 1844 when, prompted by increasing ridicule from within the mainstream churches, those remaining loyal to Adventism began to close ranks in self-defence. Indeed, they came increasingly to regard Protestantism as part of Babylon the Great, and the call to come out of Babylon added a new dimension to the missionary proclamation.

Notes

1. W. Martin and N. Klann, *Jehovah of the Watchtower*, p. 41.
2. Le Roy Edwin Froom, *The Prophetic Faith of Our Fathers*, Vol 2, pp. 195f.
3. Carl Olof Jonsson, *The Gentile Times Reconsidered*, pp. 19ff.
4. Robert Fleming, *The Rise and Fall of the Papacy*, London 1849 edition (first published 1701), p. 68. Quoted in C. O. Jonsson, p.140.
5. Ernest R. Sandeen, *The Roots of Fundamentalism*, p. 5.
6. D. W. Bebbington, *Evangelicalism in Modern Britain*, pp. 81ff.
7. H. Drummond, 'Dialogues' 1: ii-iii, quoted in E. R. Sandeen, *The Roots of Fundamentalism*, pp. 21f.
8. Sandeen, *op.cit.*, p. 57.
9. A. O. Hudson, *Bible Students in Britain*, p. 31.
10. P. Gerard Damsteegt, *Foundations of the Seventh-Day Adventist Message and Mission*, p. 4.
11. *Ibid.*, p. 6.
12. The notes on Miller and Adventism which follow are based upon P. G. Damsteegt, *Foundations of the Seventh-Day Adventist Message and Mission*. A more comprehensive history of Adventist interpretation of the prophetic material is supplied in Le Roy Edwin Froom, *The Prophetic Faith of Our Fathers*.
13. Damsteegt, *op. cit.*, pp. 16ff.
14. All Scripture quotations in this and following chapters relating to the nineteenth

and early twentieth centuries are from the King James Version, that being the version most commonly in use at the time.

15. Damsteegt, *op. cit.*, p. 24.
16. E. R. Sandeen, *op. cit.*, p. 22.
17. Uriah Smith, *Daniel and the Revelation*, p. 558.
18. *Ibid.*, pp. 561ff.

Chapter Four
Dispensationalism

The failure of William Miller's expectations in 1844 understandably left Adventism in disarray. Miller had taken the year-for-a-day principle and applied it to its uttermost. In doing so he had produced a body of teaching which exhibited a high degree of internal coherence: the time periods mentioned in the prophetic books were expounded in a consistent manner; the crucial year was identified, not by the interpretation of a single passage, but by several, all of which were derived without doing any apparent violence to the declared rules of interpretation. It is likely that the failure of such a body of teaching would have been perceived by many as a *reductio ad absurdum* of the approach to interpretation on which it was based. On the other hand, historical events did appear to confirm the correctness of the method of interpretation employed. The prophecy of the seventy weeks seemed to be confirmed by the historical facts, as did the application of the 1,260 days to the period between AD 538 and AD 1798. [1] So, although there were many who abandoned the Adventist approach to the interpretation of prophecy at this time, there were many others to whom it appeared reasonable to persevere. Nevertheless, the failure of Miller's predictions, and the aftermath of that failure, marked a significant step in the migration of historicist premillennialism to the Christian fringe.

> In both Britain and America, the millenarian revival was led by a man whose calling ultimately brought near ruin to the cause. . . . William Miller's misconception about the date of the second advent lay at the heart of his millenarian doctrine. The failure of his predictions disillusioned most of his followers and marked the whole millenarian cause, rightly or wrongly, with the stigma of fanaticism and quackery. [2]

Within the Protestant mainstream, however, a different approach to premillennialism began to gain support during the latter part of the nineteenth century. Unlike historicism, which had sought to identify historical events with the fulfilment of prophecy, the new departure rested upon the assumption that the prophecies of the second coming and the Millennium would not have their fulfilment until some unidentifiable time in the future. This futurist approach had its nineteenth-century origins with the work of S. R. Maitland who, in 1826, had published a pamphlet in which he argued against the historicist approach and the year-for-a-day principle. [3] It drew much further impetus from the ideas of John Nelson Darby (1800-1882), a minister in the Church of Ireland who was to become one of the early leaders of the Plymouth Brethren. His distinctive contribution to premillennialist speculation lay in the division of history into separate epochs or dispensations, namely: the Edenic, the Antediluvian, the Post-diluvian, the Patriarchal, the Legal, the Ecclesiastical, and the Future dispensations. Each of these epochs is characterised by the way in which God was dealing with and relating to the faithful.

This approach, though broadly similar to earlier interpretations of prophetic history, is nevertheless a product of the nineteenth century. Marsden has argued that, in providing an explanation for sudden changes in history following long periods of apparent stability, dispensationalism reflects a common preoccupation of the nineteenth century.[4] Marx's philosophy of history and the geological theory of catastrophism exemplify similar approaches to their respective disciplines. As each period in Marx's analysis ends in violent disruption, and each geological age ends in catastrophe, so with the dispensations into which religious history is divided. The Edenic dispensation ends with the Fall, the Antediluvian ends with the Flood and so on until even the Future age, the Millennium, ends when 'Satan shall be loosed out of his prison' (Revelation 20:7).

An important feature of dispensationalism, for the purposes of the present study, is a theory concerning the Ecclesiastical dispensation which allows a premillennialist interpretation of the second coming but which avoids the possibility of the sort of *reductio ad absurdum* to which Miller's approach had led. This rests upon a reinterpretation of the prophecy of the seventy weeks in Daniel 9. Miller had accepted the interpretation which applied the whole of the seventy weeks to the 490 years between the rebuilding of Jerusalem and the time of Christ. According to the reinterpretation, the Messiah was due to appear at the end of the sixty-ninth week, or 483 years following the rebuilding of Jerusalem. The final week, however, the seven years during which all remaining prophecies are to be fulfilled, did not begin immediately following the sixty-nine weeks. Rather, the Ecclesiastical dispensation has intervened and the final week is yet future. That is, the Church exists during a period to which prophecy does not apply. Prophecy is silent not only about the events of this period but also about the existence of the period itself.

The strength of Darby's dispensationalism lay in its refusal to be drawn into the kind of speculations which had previously led only to disillusionment. But that may also have been its weakness, because the enthusiasm for premillennialist ideas to which it appealed had been generated largely by the historicist approach which had prevailed until then. Within the dispensationalist systems propounded by Darby and his followers, there could be no justification for the conviction that the Ecclesiastical dispensation was nearing its close and that the second coming was imminent.

Charles Taze Russell
Towards the end of the nineteenth century, then, three main types of millennialism were in evidence. Postmillennialism, which was already well-established at the start of the century, remained healthy and reflected the continuing optimism for the gradual advancement of humanity. Among

conservative and evangelical Christians, a futurist premillennialism based upon dispensationalism had begun to gain ground. Historicist premillennialism, on the other hand, especially as represented by Adventism, remained in disarray. It is against this background that Charles Taze Russell is to be understood.

Russell was born in Pittsburgh in 1852 to Presbyterian parents. By the age of fifteen he had joined the Congregational church where he remained for a short while before becoming almost entirely sceptical of Christian belief. It was during his period as a sceptic that he first attended, in 1870, a meeting of a group which he described as 'Second Adventists' and heard Jonas Wendell expound his Adventist views. Though not convinced by Wendell's preaching, Russell's interest was kindled. He organised a small group which met regularly for Bible study between 1870 and 1875 and began to gather together the ideas which were to reach their mature systematic form in the series of volumes entitled *Millennial Dawn*. The first volume of the series, entitled *The Divine Plan of the Ages*, was published in 1886. Further volumes followed until the sixth and final one was published in 1904. Thereafter, the series was retitled *Studies in the Scriptures*. It had been Russell's hope that he would, in due course, be able to complete the series with a seventh volume dealing with the book of Revelation, but he never felt able to undertake that task. In the end it was others who, more confident than Russell in their ability to interpret the visions of Revelation, wrote what was intended to be the seventh volume following his death in 1916.

Russell's career, it should be noted, began at a very late stage in the development of historicist premillennialism. Particularly during the thirty years or so following the failure of William Miller's system, there had been much opportunity amongst continuing historicists for reflection and revision. The scope, therefore, for genuinely new ideas was limited, so caution should be exercised before the originality which is to be found in Russell's writings is attributed to Russell himself. His role was not primarily as a generator of new approaches to his subject but, rather, as the builder of a unified body of doctrine from already existing modifications of the old ideas.

In describing what he considered to be the two possible methods of attempting to seek religious truth, however, Russell could appear to the unwary to be claiming rather more originality for his ideas than is evidently the case. One method, he said,

> is to seek among all the views suggested by the various sects of the church, and to take from each that element which we might consider truth – an endless task.

This approach he rejected as leading into a

> labyrinth of bewilderment and confusion. The other method is to divest our minds of all prejudice, and to remember that none can know more about the plans of God than he has revealed in his Word, and that it was given to the meek and lowly of heart; and, as such, earnestly seeking its guidance and instruction only, we shall by its great Author be guided to an understanding of it, as it becomes due to be understood by making use of the various helps divinely provided. [5]

The impression given, then, is of a clean break with all traditions of biblical interpretation that have gone before. Russell did, indeed, claim that his approach was quite original.

> It is an examination of the subject from, so far as we know, an altogether different standpoint from that of any other work. [6]

However, he does seem to have been aware of some of the early history of the ideas upon which he drew, for he acknowledged his indebtedness to J. A. Bengel and especially to William Miller.

> A religious movement culminated in 1844, the participants in which were then, and since, generally known as 'Second Adventists' and 'Millerites,' because they expected the second advent of the Lord to occur at that date, and because a Mr William Miller was the leader and prime mover. The movement, which began about 1829, had before 1844 (when they expected the Lord's return) attracted the attention of all classes of Christian people, especially in the Eastern and Middle States where it amounted to an excitement. A long while before this, Prof. Bengel, in Tubingen (*sic*), Germany, began to call attention to the prophecies and the coming Kingdom of Messiah. [7]

> We disagree with Mr Miller's interpretations and deductions . . . yet we recognise that movement as being in God's order, and as doing a very important work in the separating, purifying, refining, and thus making ready, of a waiting people prepared for the Lord. [8]

As this study proceeds, it will become evident that Russell was greatly indebted to his predecessors.

The Divine Plan of the Ages

The first volume of *Studies in the Scriptures*, despite the claim to originality noted above, is a reworking of a modified dispensationalism expounded by Russell's early associate, Nelson H. Barbour, a former associate of Miller, in his book, *Three Worlds and the Harvest of This World*. Although that book was written entirely by Barbour, its title page bears Russell's name as co-author,[9] but it is perhaps no longer possible to determine the extent of Russell's contribution to the theory. All that can be reasonably certain is that in *The Divine Plan of the Ages* Russell expounded a version of dispensationalism which had its origins within the millennialist circles with which he was first associated.

It would be misleading to describe Russell's system as dispensationalist without qualification; his ideas follow closely in succession to those of Miller and not those of Darby. But his classification of religious history into dispensations does appear, at first glance, to be borrowed in its entirety from Darby. Russell's modifications, however, are far-reaching and do more than simply adapt dispensationalism to a historicist premillennialist system; they create from it a fundamental component of the new system.

Religious history is divided into three great epochs, or worlds: the first epoch, or 'the world that was', extends from creation to the Flood; the second epoch is the 'present evil world' which extends from the Flood until the dawn of the third epoch, 'the world to come'. During the first epoch the world was under the ministration of angels; during the second epoch Satan has limited control; the third epoch will be under divine administration. The second epoch is further subdivided into three ages or dispensations: the Patriarchal, the Jewish and the Gospel ages. The world to come is similarly subdivided but in that case there is information concerning its first constituent age only, the Millennial age.[10]

So far, what has been described could have come from any one of Darby's many successors. As Russell's ideas are developed, however, fundamental differences become apparent. Firstly, it should be noted that Russell maintained a traditional historicist interpretation of Daniel's prophecy of the seventy weeks. Consequently, in his 'Plan of the Ages' the Gospel age does not occupy a hiatus in prophetic time. Secondly, according to Russell, the ages overlap: the Gospel age has its beginning in stages, first with the baptism of Jesus and later at Pentecost; similarly the Jewish age closes in stages, first with Jesus' rejection of the Jews, 'Your house is left unto you desolate' (Matthew 23:38), and more completely with the taking of the Gospel to the Gentiles, beginning with Cornelius (Acts 10:45).[11] Likewise, the Gospel age closes and the Millennial age begins in stages – a fact which adds piquancy to Russell's proclamation of the end of the Gospel age, for it means that the Millennium has actually begun. It is this fact that was alluded to in the original title of his series, *Millennial Dawn*. Far from avoiding the potential pitfalls inherent in historicist premillennialism, then, Russell's adaptation of dispensationalism provided a further means whereby the end-time calendar might be compiled, as will become apparent in due course.

The function of the Gospel proclamation during the Gospel age is not to convert the world to Christianity but, rather, to select the 'little flock' (Luke 12:32). This 'little flock' constitutes the whole of the Church, not a part of it; in comparison with the 'nominal Church' it is very small indeed, comprising only 144,000 members (Revelation 7:4).[12] It should not be inferred from this, however, that Russell believed only a small proportion of mankind would be saved. That would be to confuse what belongs to one dispensation with what belongs to another. To fail to be elected to the 'high calling' of the true Church is not thereby to be damned, for judgement belongs to the Millennial age. It is not until the 'Day' of Judgement, which will occupy the whole of the Millennium, that the vast majority of humanity will be required to make their final response to the Gospel – indeed, they will not be able to make such response until then.

During the closing years of the Gospel age, then, the Lord is at work in the world making up the final number of the 'little flock'. These are the ones who will share with Christ the divine nature, and will have a part in judging all mankind during the Millennium. It is only to the members of the 'little flock' that the Holy Spirit is given during the Gospel age and consequently it is only they who are able to appreciate the Gospel and respond appropriately. In the coming age God will 'pour out his spirit upon all flesh' (Joel 2:28). Then, and not before, mankind generally will be in a position to make a proper response to the Gospel, and it will be by their actions then, not now, that they will be judged.[13] Before that, none, other than the members of the 'little flock,' have sufficient light for their actions to merit the final penalty, the 'second death'.[14]

God's plan for the coming Millennial age is the restoration of the world to the perfection that was lost in Eden.[15] Jesus' sacrificial death provides a ransom for all, but that does not guarantee that all shall have everlasting life. Rather, it guarantees that all shall have a second chance, under perfect conditions, to prove their obedience to the divine will. That is, early in the Millennial age all are to be resurrected into surroundings comparable with those of Adam and Eve; the same divine requirement of absolute obedience will apply then as applied in Eden, but the subjects of the Millennial Kingdom will have the great advantage of vastly increased knowledge.[16]

During this period of judgement all the members of the 'little flock' will be in heaven where they are to share in the divine nature. They, under Christ, are the heavenly judges. Assisting in their work, as it were, is another class who are to be resurrected to the earth in order to carry out the great educational work that judgement requires. These are the 'ancient worthies', or those who have been selected during the pre-Christian ages in a way roughly analogous to that in which the 'little flock' are selected. At the end of the Millennium they are to be removed from earth to heaven where they partake, not in the divine nature like the 'little flock', but in the same spiritual nature as the angels. By that time the majority of mankind will have attained perfect humanity and will receive the reward of everlasting human life on earth.

The 'Plan of the Ages' has more significance in Russell's system than as simply the classification of periods of religious history. It will become clear later that his belief in parallels, or correspondences, between the Jewish and the Gospel ages allowed him to generate corroborative arguments in support of his interpretation of prophecy. Further, as will become apparent in due course, the significance of some of the revisions which were made to the system following Russell's death is seen in relation to the distinctive line of argument deriving from the 'Plan of the Ages,' and its eventual disappearance from Watch Tower millennialism.

Notes

1. In addition to the events mentioned during the course of the exposition of Miller's ideas in Chapter Two, the fall of the Ottoman Empire had also provided apparent confirmation of this approach. Writing in 1838, Josiah Litch had interpreted 'an hour, and a day, and a month, and a year' (Revelation 9:15) on the basis of the year-for-a-day principle. The 391 years and 15 days which he thus calculated he applied to the duration of the Ottoman Empire. The supremacy of Islam over the Greeks was established on 27 July 1449, so the Ottoman Empire was due to come to an end on 11 August 1840. 'The time set for the fulfilment of the prophecy . . . was watched by thousands with intense interest. And the exact accomplishment of the event predicted, showing, as it did, the right application of the prophecy, gave a mighty impetus to the great Advent movement then beginning to attract the attention of the world.' (Uriah Smith, *Daniel and the Revelation*, pp. 456ff.)

2. E. R. Sandeen, *The Roots of Fundamentalism*, p. 58.

3. D. W. Bebbington, *Evangelicalism in Modern Britain*, pp. 85f.

4. G. M. Marsden, *Fundamentalism and American Culture*, pp. 64ff. See also T. P. Weber, *Living in the Shadow of the Second Coming; American Premillennialism*

1875-1925.
5.C. T. Russell, *The Divine Plan of the Ages*, pp. 11f.
6.*Ibid.*, p. 13.
7.C. T. Russell, *Thy Kingdom Come*, p. 84.
8.*Ibid.*, p. 86.
9.M. J. Penton, *Apocalypse Delayed,* p. 19.
10.C. T. Russell, *The Divine Plan of the Ages*, pp. 70ff.
11.Ibid., p. 223f.
12.C. T. Russell, *The New Creation*, p. 179.
13.C. T. Russell, *The Divine Plan of the Ages* ., pp. 86ff.
14.*Ibid.*, p. 145.
15.*Ibid.*, p. 149.
16.*Ibid.*, p. 151.

Chapter Five
The Time is at Hand

In *The Time is at Hand*, the second volume of *Studies in the Scriptures*, Russell set out to demonstrate that the various features of the 'Plan of the Ages' must all take place according to a divinely predetermined timetable. His object was

> to make plain upon tables that which God said would be sealed up,
> and which therefore could not be understood before this time of the
> end, but of which he gave assurance that it should *then* be understood.[1]

His approach to the interpretation of prophecy employed two basic methods: the year-for-a-day rule, which was already a well established principle within the tradition which he inherited; and the idea of prophetic parallels which, though by no means original, receives a distinctive treatment in Russell's hands.

It is in the nature of historicist premillennialism that the logical character of interpretive systems should reflect their historical relation to the prophetic fulfilments which they purport to describe. Thus it was noted above[2] that the logical sequence of Miller's thought differed from that of most of his eighteenth-century predecessors in the tradition by taking the end point of the 1,260 days, rather than its beginning, as the first fixed point upon which the argument is constructed. Turning to Russell's treatment of the prophetic material, a further similar shift becomes apparent. From Joachim onwards, premillennialism had looked forward to the end of the 1,260 days and to the second coming of Christ; Miller looked back upon the end of the 1,260 days and forward to the second coming; Russell looks back upon both these events and forward to their consequences.

That Russell believed he could look back to Christ's second coming indicates a very different idea of what such a momentous event involves from that of his Adventist predecessors. Their mistake, he believed, was that they had 'not been expecting to see him as he is, but as he was'.[3] They had assumed that his coming (Greek: *parousia*) was to be a single event. For Russell, however, '*parousia*' is understood as meaning, not simply 'coming' or 'return', but as implying Christ's continuing presence following his return. The word is therefore rendered 'presence' throughout Russell's writings and in all subsequent Watch Tower literature. At his return Christ is invisibly present; the moment of his arrival may pass unnoticed, but the fact of his presence will become more and more evident until at last it is inescapable.[4] That Christ is invisibly present is recognisable by two means: it becomes evident from study of the prophetic material as interpreted by Russell; and eventually it will become evident to mankind in general when people begin to realise the significance of developments in international affairs. Russell's characterisation of Christ's return, then, has elements in common with that of James Hatley Frere earlier in the nineteenth century.[5]

At this point it may fairly be asked whether Russell believed that Christ was to be literally, though invisibly, present in the earth from the beginning of the Parousia or at any time during it. The question, however, is one which he does not address. He appears to equate literal presence with visible presence. If this is correct, then in ruling out the latter, he rules out the former also. Certainly, present-day Watch Tower doctrine, which describes Christ's presence during the Parousia in terms of his directing his attention towards the earth, and which denies any literal presence whether visible or invisible,[6] is consistent with Russell's views as expressed in *The Time is at Hand*. The modern doctrine, where Russell was vague, is explicit in its denial of any literal presence.

The Seventy Weeks

The point of departure for Russell's exposition of the prophetic material is Daniel's prophecy of the seventy weeks 'unto Messiah the Prince' (Daniel 9:24-27). This is the paradigm case of the application of the year-for-a-day rule.

> While many prophecies combine to fix and confirm the date of the second coming of Christ, this one alone marked the date of the first advent. If its fulfilment is clearly established, it will aid us in calculating and judging of those relating to the second advent.[7]

By the late nineteenth century two basic approaches to the prophecy of the seventy weeks were established. The first is exemplified by the Adventist interpretation, a refinement of the relatively simple approach which Miller had followed in applying the whole of the seventy weeks to the period extending from the decree of Artaxerxes for the rebuilding of Jerusalem to the crucifixion of Jesus. This refinement takes note of the fact that Messiah is said to cause the cessation of the sacrifice and oblation (that is, by his sacrificial death which fulfils the ancient prophetic type) in 'the midst of the week' (Daniel 9:27). So, from the date of the decree to rebuild Jerusalem to the beginning of Christ's ministry is sixty-nine weeks, or 483 years from 457 BC to AD 27; to his crucifixion is a further half week, or three and a half years, to A.D. 31; and from the start of his ministry 'he shall confirm the covenant with many for one week' (Daniel 9:27). That is, from the beginning of Jesus' ministry there is a period of seven years during which the Old Covenant with the Jewish people is confirmed as remaining in force. Throughout this period the Gospel is taken exclusively to the Jews. The period ends in AD 34 when the martyrdom of Stephen marks the final formal rejection of the Gospel by the Jewish Sanhedrin. Thereafter the apostles turn their attention to the Gentiles.[8]

The second major approach to the interpretation of the seventy weeks was that followed by the dispensationalist movement in which the sixty-nine weeks extended to the coming of Messiah and the Ecclesiastical dispensation intervenes before the eventual completion of the whole period of seventy weeks.

Both these interpretations recognise a reference in the prophecy to a second prince. The Adventist view is that the words 'the prince that shall come shall destroy the city and the sanctuary' (Daniel 9:26) refer to the destruction of Jerusalem by the Romans in AD 70. In verse 27 the reference reverts to Messiah and indicates the effective end of the Jewish sacrificial system by Christ's crucifixion: 'he shall cause the sacrifice and oblation to cease'. Thereafter 'he shall make it desolate', by which is meant that divine favour is removed from the Jewish nation as the Gospel is taken to the Gentiles. In the dispensationalist view, on the other hand, the second prince mentioned in the prophecy is Antichrist who is to appear during the seventieth week. Causing the sacrifice and oblation to cease indicates Antichrist's attack upon pure worship which is the start of the 'great tribulation'.

Russell's exposition of the seventy weeks is identical in all important respects to that of his Adventist contemporary, Uriah Smith. The period begins to count from the decree of Artaxerxes to rebuild Jerusalem, but Russell took 454 BC as the date of that decree. Jesus' ministry begins in AD 29 at the end of the sixty-ninth week, and his crucifixion occurs at the mid-point of the seventieth week. For seven years following the start of Jesus' ministry the Covenant with the Jewish nation remains in force; its end is signified three-and-a-half years after Jesus' death by the conversion of Cornelius in AD 36 and the subsequent taking of the Gospel to the Gentiles.[9]

By this exposition, Russell established the way in which prophecy relates to the first advent and justified his use of the year-for-a-day rule. He has established some important dates which will be needed later in connection with prophecies relating to the second advent. Although the dates, which are crucial within each variation of the application of the seventy weeks, are by no means all securely fixed by historical scholarship, it should be appreciated that all the variations come sufficiently close to the historical facts to lend credibility to the procedure adopted.[10] Consequently, if subsequent applications of the method to other prophetic material should not be confirmed by the course of events, it is only those particular applications which are thereby seen to fail. The method itself appears to have already received adequate confirmation, so the possibility of revision of details where necessary will remain open.

The Times of the Gentiles

Russell's next applications of the year-for-a-day rule show the influence of two of his predecessors, William Miller and John Aquila Brown. First, he gives pride of place to what had been, for Miller, a secondary indicator of the due time for Christ's return, and which had been discarded by later Adventism. Miller had believed that the reference in Leviticus 26 to chastisement of the people of Israel 'seven times' for their sins, indicated a period of 2,520 years. This, he maintained, extended from the time of the taking of the first exiles from Jerusalem to Babylon in 677 BC until AD 1843. The Adventist writer and commentator, Uriah Smith, rejected this for the reason that 'seven times' must here be understood not as indicating seven years, whether calendar years or prophetic years, but as 'simply an adverb expressing degree'.[11]

In Russell's system, Miller's interpretation of Leviticus 26:27-33 is reinstated and amended. The seven times, or seven prophetic years of 360 days each, represent 2,520 years, but the period begins, not with the taking of the first exiles to Babylon, but with the ending of the typical Kingdom of God and the consequent lease of universal dominion to Gentile governments. This signal event had been foretold by Ezekiel:

> Thou, profane wicked prince of Israel, whose day is come, when iniquity shall have an end, thus saith the Lord God; remove the diadem, and take off the crown: this shall not be the same: exalt him that is low, and abase him that is high. I will overturn, overturn, overturn, it: and it shall be no more, until he come whose right it is; and I will give it him. (Ezekiel 21:25-27)

Nebuchadnezzar laid siege to Jerusalem, deposed Zedekiah, and so there began both the full Jewish exile and the 'times of the Gentiles' (Luke 21:24). This occurred in 606 BC. This date, though not attested by historical scholarship, is not arbitrarily chosen. It is calculated from the well attested date of the restoration during the first year of Cyrus, 536 BC, on the assumption that Jerusalem had remained desolate for seventy years during the exile (2 Chronicles 36:21). The 'times of the Gentiles' therefore extend to 1914.[12]

It is important to note that although the Babylonian exile came to an end and Jerusalem and the temple were rebuilt, the Davidic monarchy was never restored. The typical Kingdom of God had ceased to exist. This was not, however, a violation of the promise that

> the sceptre shall not depart from Judah, nor a lawgiver from between his feet, until Shiloh come. (Genesis 49:10)

The sceptre and the crown are to be distinguished. The crown represents the power to govern, which was indeed taken away from Zedekiah, but the sceptre represents the right to govern. The right, though not the power, to govern remained with Judah until the time of Jesus who 'became the rightful and only heir of the long-promised scepter of earth'. Jesus received the sceptre at his resurrection but this does not mean that the Kingdom of God had its beginning then; it was only very much later that he was to take up the power of the kingdom.[13]

The beginning of the 'times of the Gentiles' marks the end of the typical Kingdom of God, the Kingdom of Israel, but the end of that period should not be straightforwardly identified with the inauguration of the antitypical kingdom. As will be seen later, Russell believed that the Kingdom of God was established in heaven in 1874. The end of the 'times of the Gentiles' is the due date for the establishment of the kingdom on the earth, an event which is intimately connected with the fortunes of the Jewish nation.

> The world is witness to the fact that Israel's punishment under the dominion of the Gentiles has been continuous since B.C. 606, that it still continues, and that there is no reason to expect their national re-organisation sooner than A.D. 1914, the limit of their 'seven times' - 2520 years. But as this long period of their national chastisement draws near its close, we can see marked indications that the barren fig tree is about to put forth, showing that the winter time of evil is closing, and the Millennial summer approaching, which will fully restore them to

their promised inheritance and national independence. The fact that there are now great preparations and expectations relative to the return of Israel to their own land is of itself strong circumstantial evidence corroborative of this Scripture teaching.[14]

Russell has a second derivation of the 2,520 year period and it is here that Brown's influence is apparent. Brown, about whom little is known, had derived the 2,520 years from an interpretation of Daniel 4, as early as 1823, and had identified them with the period from 604 BC to AD 1917, though he had not equated this with the 'times of the Gentiles' of Luke 21:24.[15] With relatively minor amendments, Brown's ideas were incorporated into Russell's system. The 'times of the Gentiles', then, constitute not only a period of punishment for the nation of Israel; they are also a period of degradation for mankind in general. This is indicated in Daniel 4, which describes Nebuchadnezzar's dream of a great tree which is cut down and restrained from growth for seven years before being allowed to flourish once more. According to Daniel, the dream indicates a period of seven years' humiliation for Nebuchadnezzar, after which he is to be restored to his former position. For Russell this dream has a greater prophetic significance, namely, the general human degradation which is to characterise the 'times of the Gentiles':

> Unless it was thus to foreshow the degradation and the duration of Gentile Times, we know of no reason for the recording of this scrap of history of a heathen king. That his seven years of degradation fitly illustrated human debasement, is a fact; that God has promised a restitution of earth's dominion after humanity has learned certain great lessons, is also a fact; and that the seven symbolic times (2520 years) end at the exact point when mankind will have learned its own degradation and present inability to rule the world to advantage, and will be ready for God's kingdom and dominion, is a third fact.[16]

In so far as the 'times of the Gentiles' are a punishment upon the Jewish people, their ending will be marked by the return of the Jews to Palestine. The government which they will then establish will be the beginning of the Kingdom of God on earth and it will rapidly replace all other national governments (Daniel 2:44). In so far as the 'times of the Gentiles' are a period of general human degradation, their end will be marked by the enlightenment of mankind. And that enlightenment will culminate in the acknowledgement that the government which by that time will be established in Jerusalem for the repatriated Jewish nation, is actually of divine origin; all national governments will at last submit to the authority of the theocratic kingdom.

Earth's Great Jubilee

The Time is at Hand continues with the reinstatement and amendment of the next of Miller's two secondary indicators of the due date for the beginning of the Millennium which, like the identification of the 'times of the Gentiles', had been discarded by later Adventism. Though advising caution when looking for prophetic types in Scripture, Russell expresses confidence when dealing with those areas which he does regard as typical or prophetic:

> On no such unsafe ground do we build when examining the ceremonies of the Jewish Law, given specially as types and declared by the apostles to be such. Nor can we afford to let these types pass without due

consideration and careful study of the lessons they teach, any more than we can afford to spend time in speculating, and in building faith upon mere conjecture.[17]

The prophetic significance of the Jubilee in Russell's system, then, is by no means secondary. The ancient Jewish Law provided for a series of sabbaths, the greatest of which was the fiftieth year, the Jubilee year. The primary purpose of the Jubilee was restoration: slaves were to be given their liberty, and property, which could not be sold in perpetuity but only leased for the duration of the time remaining until the next Jubilee, was to be returned to its rightful owners (Leviticus 25:10-15).

> This arrangement provided by God through their leader and typical mediator, Moses, though itself a blessed boon, foreshadowed a still greater blessing which God had in view – the release of all mankind from the debt of sin and its bondage and servitude, through Christ our Lord, the greater Mediator and Deliverer, whom Moses typified. (Deut 18:15) It was thus, in types, that Moses wrote of Christ and the blessings to come through him (John 5:46; 1:45) – the Great Restitution and Jubilee to come to all the race, now groaning under the bondage of corruption and slavery to sin.[18]

The significance of the Jubilee, then, is the same for Russell as it had been for Miller; Russell's arithmetic, however, is somewhat different. Where Miller had assumed that the Millennium, as the antitypical Jubilee, must take the place of the fiftieth fifty-year period, Russell believed that it was to take the place of the actual fiftieth Jubilee only. He, therefore, counted 2,499 years from the cessation of the type to the inauguration of the antitype, where Miller had counted 2,450 years. Where Miller had straightforwardly identified the cessation of the type with the beginning of the Babylonian exile, Russell believed that it was necessary to identify the final Jubilee year to be observed prior to the exile. This, he calculated, occurred nineteen years before the exile. Simple arithmetic, then, fixed 1874 as the year when the Millennium was due to begin.

His calculation was as follows: from the entry into Canaan until the Babylonian exile was 969 years. This allowed the celebration of nineteen Jubilees, leaving a balance of nineteen years. Since the Jubilee regulations came into effect immediately upon entry into Canaan and the fifty-year cycles began to count from that time, it follows that the whole of this balance of nineteen years must have come after the final Jubilee. That the last Jubilee prior to the exile was, indeed, the final Jubilee is indicated by the fact that the exile lasted for 70 years during which time a Jubilee must have come due, but could not have been observed outside of Canaan. The whole sequence of typical Jubilees, then, has come to a halt. Therefore, the great cycle of fifty times fifty years, which precedes the antitypical Jubilee, began to count from nineteen years before the exile. So, this 19 years, plus 70 years of exile, plus 536 years BC following the exile (536 being the date of Cyrus's decree to rebuild Jerusalem) give a total of 625 years. This is the proportion of the 2,500 which falls before AD 1. Subtracting 625 from 2,500 gives 1,875. That is, AD 1875 is the final year of the great cycle. Instead of being a one-year Jubilee, however, it is replaced by the great antitype, the Millennium which, therefore, begins at the end of AD 1874.[19]

Restoration

For Russell, the beginning of the Millennium, the antitypical Jubilee, marks also the beginning of the second presence of Christ.

> 'He shall send Jesus Christ, which before was preached unto you, whom the heaven must retain *until* THE TIMES OF RESTITUTION OF ALL THINGS, which God hath spoken by the mouth of all his holy prophets since the world began.' – Acts 3:19-21. On the strength of this inspired statement alone, we have clear evidence of the fact that our Lord's second advent *was due* when the Times of Restitution *were due* to begin, viz., in October, A D 1874, as marked by the Jubilee arrangement.[20]

But the earliest years of the Millennium are not marked by the cataclysmic changes which other millennialists had expected. Indeed, the restoration of mankind to Edenic perfection is gradual and, at first, imperceptible to all but the few who have understood the significance of the old prophecies. The Millennial Dawn is marked by reforms in political, social, economic and industrial life; the campaigners for such reforms are, for the most part, unaware of the real motivation underlying their efforts.

> None but the Lord's 'little flock' is fully and correctly informed as to the grand scope of the Restitution. These see the minor changes, the straightening out of the lesser affairs of men, but they see also what can be seen from no other standpoint than God's Word - that the great enslaver, Sin, is to be shorn of his power, that the great prison-house of Death is to be opened and a release presented to each prisoner, signed in the precious blood of the Lamb of God which taketh away the sin of the world, the great Redeemer and Restorer. Glad tidings indeed it shall be to all people, not only to the living, but also to all that are in their graves. Before the end of this great Jubilee every human being may go entirely free - may get back to man's first estate, 'very good,' receiving back through Christ all that was lost in Adam.[21]

The gradual nature of the early stages of millennial restitution which Russell envisaged, fostered a resilience within the Watch Tower movement without which it might not have been possible to survive the disappointment of 1914. Cataclysmic changes had, indeed, been expected for that year but the movement had lived with forty years of gradual change and gathering momentum. That more of the same sort of thing was still necessary, following the Millennium's first phase, did not require too great a revision of beliefs – for a time, at least.

Notes

1. C. T. Russell, *The Time is at Hand*, p. 15.
2. Above, Chapter 3.
3. Russell, *op. cit.*, p. 29.
4. *Ibid.*, p. 107.
5. Above, Chapter 3.

6. Anon., *You Can Live Forever in Paradise on Earth*, p. 147.

7. Russell, *op. cit.*, p. 64.

8. U. Smith, *Daniel and the Revelation*, pp. 189ff.

9. Russell, *op. cit.*, pp. 66ff.

10. Modern scholarship generally applies the seventy weeks to the period between the exile and the death of Antiochus Epiphanes in 164 BC (N. Porteous, *Daniel: A Commentary*, p.141). Such an explanation is unlikely to commend itself to the millennialist mind, however, since the chronological fit of this approach is so far from exact as to be entirely at odds with the assumption of historical accuracy in Scripture.

11. Smith, *op. cit.*, p. 693.

12. Russell, *op. cit.*, pp. 78ff.

13. *Ibid.*, pp. 82ff.

14. *Ibid.*, pp. 92f.

15. M. J. Penton, *Apocalypse Delayed*, p. 21.

16. Russell, *op. cit.*, p. 97.

17. *Ibid.*, p. 174.

18. *Ibid.*, p. 177.

19. *Ibid.*, pp. 184ff.

20. *Ibid.*, p. 188.

21. *Ibid.*, pp. 199f.

Chapter Six
Parallel Dispensations

The foregoing sections have described the basic outline of Russell's dispensational theory, and have begun to identify some significant years in the unfolding of prophetic history. Returning now to the 'Plan of the Ages', it becomes apparent, upon further examination, that the Plan itself has a prophetic significance which had not been part of Darby's theory or that of any of his successors. In fact, the added significance of the dispensations is an extension of the idea of prophetic types:

> In this chapter we purpose to show that the whole Jewish nation, during that entire age, was unwittingly engaged, under God's direction, in furnishing for our instruction a typical view of the entire plan of salvation in all its workings, even as we have just seen its Jubilees pointing out the final consummation of the plan.[1]

It is not simply that events which befell the Jewish nation during the Jewish age were prophetic counterparts of events to befall the Church during the Gospel age, the timing of those events also had prophetic significance:

> Not only were Fleshly Israel and its ceremonies typical, but the Jewish *age* was typical of the Gospel *age*. They are of exactly the same length, and correspond to each other; so that, seeing and appreciating the Jewish age, its length, and the peculiarities of its harvest or close, we may know the exact length of the Gospel age, its antitype, and may understand what to look for, and when, in the harvest of the Gospel age.[2]

The first step in Russell's proof that the two ages or dispensations are parallel is found in Paul's letter to the Romans:

> For I would not, brethren, that ye should be ignorant of this mystery, lest ye should be wise in your own conceits; that blindness in part is happened to Israel, until the fulness of the Gentiles be come in. And so all Israel shall be saved: as it is written, there shall come out of Sion the Deliverer, and shall turn away ungodliness from Jacob: For this is my covenant unto them, when I shall take away their sins. (Romans 11:25-27)

Here Paul indicates that the Jewish nation, fleshly Israel, has been cast off from divine favour during the time that spiritual Israel, the Church, or 'little flock', is being selected. When the full number of the Church has been completed, fleshly Israel will be restored to divine favour. For the next step in the argument, to indicate the timing of the close of the Gospel age, Russell draws upon Peter's speech to a Jewish audience at Solomon's Colonnade:

> Repent ye therefore, and be converted, that your sins may be blotted out, when the times of refreshing shall come from the presence of the Lord. (Acts 3:19)

Taking these two passages of Scripture together, Russell draws from Paul the conclusion that the return to favour of the Jewish nation will be when God takes away their sin, and from Peter he draws the conclusion that this is to occur at the times of refreshing or restitution, that is, at the Lord's second presence.[3]

Now, it has already been shown that the date of the second presence of Christ and the beginning of the times of restitution is AD 1874. So, shortly thereafter it may be expected that some indications of the return of divine favour to fleshly Israel will become apparent, and Russell was, indeed, convinced that such indications were there to be found. First, however, it should be noted that the time of Israel's return to favour has only been roughly shown, for the time of special favour towards the Gentiles ends

> *in* the beginning of the Times of Restitution; but not (other prophecies show) *at* the very beginning of it.[4]

To fill in the details in this part of the 'Plan of the Ages,' Russell begins with the observation that the nation of Israel enjoyed special favour from God for a period of eighteen hundred and forty-five years. This spans the period from the death of Jacob until the year AD 33 when, five days before his crucifixion, Jesus signalled the Jews' casting-off in the words 'Behold, your house is left unto you desolate' (Matthew 23:38).

Their fall from favour, however, was not an instantaneous event but progressed for thirty-seven years until AD 70, when Jerusalem was destroyed by the Roman armies and the Jewish fall was complete. It should be noted, however, that although the nation's fall began in AD 33 God's favour continued towards individual Jews for three-and-a-half years following Pentecost, during which time the Gospel was proclaimed exclusively to Jews.

These details of the Jewish fall from divine favour, it will be remembered, are drawn from Russell's exposition of the the prophecy of the seventy weeks of Daniel 9.[5] So his treatment of the parallel dispensations, in effect, extends the significance of the seventieth week of Daniel's prophecy from the first advent alone to the second also.

Before proceeding to a consideration of the events which mark the close of the Gospel age, however, it is necessary to see how Russell seeks to prove that the two ages are of equal duration. This he does by reference to a prophecy from Jeremiah:

> Therefore I will cast you out of this land into a land that ye know not, neither ye nor your fathers; and there shall ye serve other gods day and night; where I will not shew you favour. (Jeremiah 16:13)

This prophecy cannot have its fulfilment in any of the early exiles, in Syria,

Babylon, or surrounding lands, for these lands were known to the Jewish people or their ancestors. The reference therefore has to be to their dispersion and fall from favour following the time of Christ. Further, the prophecy states: 'I will recompense their iniquity and their sin double' (Jeremiah 16:18).

The Hebrew word here rendered 'double' is *mishneh*, and signifies a second portion, a repetition. Thus understood, the Prophet's declaration is, that from the time of their being cast off from all favor until the time of their return to favor, would be a repetition, or *duplication in time*, of their previous history, during which time they had enjoyed divine favor.[6]

It is now possible to complete the calculations. It has already been shown that the period of divine favour towards the Jewish nation was eighteen hundred and forty-five years from the death of Jacob to their rejection in AD 33. Their *double*, or repetition of the same period without favour, then, extends from AD 33 until AD 1878. This is the year when the Jewish people are restored to divine favour.[7]

In setting out Russell's arguments concerning the due date for the restoration of the Jewish people to divine favour, it will have become apparent that we are dealing with an approach to the interpretation of Scripture which, though superficially similar to that which depends upon identifying types and antitypes, is really rather different. Israel's fall from divine favour between AD 33 and AD 70 points forward prophetically to her restoration to favour between AD 1878 and AD 1914. But it is not a straightforward instance of type and antitype, for in each case it is Israel that we are concerned with. However, there is, overlaid upon this prophetic calendar, another which is of the more familiar type and antitype variety. That is, whilst Israel's affairs during the first century foreshadow her affairs during the nineteenth and twentieth centuries, they also foreshadow the affairs of that which she typifies, namely, spiritual Israel both nominal and faithful. By nominal spiritual Israel, Russell meant Christendom in general, whereas spiritual Israel properly so called, indicates the 'elect', the 'body of Christ', which is the true Church. So the enquiry turns now to what is indicated for each of the groups represented in the prophetic material.

Fleshly Israel at the End of the Gospel Age

Russell believed that he found confirmation of his theories in current affairs. Evidence that God's favour was, indeed, returning to fleshly Israel was seen in the fact that Jewish people were at last allowed privileges in Palestine which had been denied them for centuries. Most striking was the fact that in 1878, the very year when divine favour was due to be restored, the Berlin Congress of Nations was held in which Lord Beaconsfield, who was Jewish, was the central figure. That Congress brought the Asiatic provinces of Turkey, among which was Palestine, under a British protectorate. The Turkish Government passed amendments to its laws concerning aliens which ameliorated the condition of Jewish residents in Palestine, and began to open the doors for other Jewish people to settle there and to own property, a right previously denied them. At the same time that all this was happening, there began fierce persecution of Jews in Romania, Germany and Russia. Paradoxically, this also was a mark of returning divine favour towards them, for its result would be to increase the tendency amongst Jewish people to look to their ancient heritage.[8] 1878, however, was but the turning point in Jewish affairs. It has already been shown[9] that fleshly Israel's national punishment is to continue for a period of 2,520 years, which was not due to expire until 1914. Greater and more compelling signs that divine favour had been restored were to be expected as that year approached with its culmination in the full restoration of the Jews to Palestine in readiness for the establishment of the earthly phase of the Kingdom of God.[10]

Christendom and the Elect at the End of the Gospel Age

The fate of Christendom, or nominal Christianity, cannot be separated from the blessings for the Elect, or the true Church, during this period. Both follow from the response to the presence of Christ: nominal Christianity fails to recognise his presence and is therefore rejected; the true Church hails Christ as king and is therefore blessed. This corresponds exactly with major events during Jesus' earthly ministry: just before his crucifixion he presented himself to the Jewish people as their king, pronounced judgement upon them, and threw the traders out of the Temple (Luke 19:28-48). All this took place three-and-a-half years after his ministry had begun. These events and their timing, together with the argument demonstrating that the Jewish and Gospel ages are parallel to each other, enabled Russell to enter some considerable detail into his end-time calendar.

The argument from parallel dispensations, then, fixed the beginning of Christ's second presence 1,845 years after his baptism and the beginning of his earthly ministry, and confirmed the argument from the Jubilees that this took place in 1874. At that point, corresponding to the beginning of the Harvest of the Jewish age, there began the forty-year period of the Harvest of the Gospel age.[11] Three and a half years later, in 1878, came the events prefigured by Jesus' triumphal entry into Jerusalem, his rejection of the Jewish people, and his turning the traders out of the temple. That is, 1878 was the year when Christ actually assumed the office of king and the

> nominal church systems were 'spewed out' (Rev. 3:16), and from which time they are not the mouth pieces of God, nor in any degree recognised by him.[12]

As the fall from favour of fleshly Israel was a gradual process lasting thirty-seven years, so the fall of Christendom was to be progressive, culminating in her complete destruction immediately following 1914.

For three and a half years following the beginning of fleshly Israel's fall from divine favour as a nation, favour continued to be extended to individual Jews in that the Gospel was preached exclusively to them. This continuing privilege came to an end in AD 36 with the conversion of Cornelius and the beginning of the mission to the Gentiles. That event has its end-time counterpart in 1881 with the close of the 'high calling' or invitation to become joint heirs with Christ. But this does not indicate that from that year there is no further necessity for the proclamation of the Gospel, for those who are called are not automatically chosen. In the time remaining to them they must make good their response to the call.

One further date requires attention in order to complete that part of the calendar which derives from the parallelism between the Jewish and Gospel ages. That is the date thirty years before Jesus' baptism, or his anointing as Messiah, and the beginning of his ministry. Scripture indicates that at the time of Jesus' birth faithful Jews were already expecting the Messiah (Luke 3:15). They were, in fact, thirty years premature. This circumstance also has its nineteenth-century parallel, for it was in 1844 that William Miller's movement anticipated the second coming of Christ, exactly thirty years before the actual event.[13] This observation by Russell is one of the clearest indications that he believed early nineteenth-century Adventism to be an integral part of the same overall movement to which he himself belonged.

A First Appraisal

It is appropriate to pause at this stage in order to make a preliminary assessment of Russell's millennialist system as outlined so far. Although there is much substance and detail yet to be added to the foregoing, what has been described so far could be regarded as a virtually complete body of millennialist doctrine. Indeed, so to regard it is illuminating.

This abbreviated system can be described as follows: it comprises an end-time calendar consisting of two independently established end points and a sequence of events which is, again, independently established. The starting date in the calendar, 1874, rests upon the calculation of the Jubilees; the end point, 1914 rests upon two different ways of calculating the 'times of the Gentiles'; and the sequence of events between those points is established by the argument from the parallel dispensations. Given the assumptions from which all these arguments proceed, the whole system hangs together coherently, each part of it supported not only by its own direct argument, but drawing confirmation from the rest of the system.

Two observations are worth making at this point. First, considering only this abbreviated system, then Russell's claim to originality which was noted above[14] – for the system which he expounded, not necessarily for his own contribution to it – appears to be justified. Though the elements are drawn from earlier millennialist writers, Russell's use of them is distinctive. In his treatment of what had been subsidiary indicators of the end time for William Miller, Russell does considerably more than lift the arguments from the Jubilees and the 'times of the Gentiles' from their position in an appendix into the main body of his text. They are of major significance in his system. And his adaptation of Darby's dispensationalism, far from being a way of retaining millennialist beliefs without the need to construct an end-time calendar, is central to his process of identifying due dates for prophetic fulfilments.

My second observation concerns the way in which Russell's system might be categorised. It is, clearly, a historicist version of millennialism and when consideration is given to Russell's interpretation of the prophecies of Daniel, such a categorisation will appear beyond question. At this stage in the exposition of his system, however, distinct echoes of some elements of futurism are apparent. Characteristic of the futurism of Darby was the intervention of the Gospel age between the Jewish age and the final week of Daniel's prophecy of the seventy weeks. Something of the sort is evident in Russell: the Gospel age intervenes between the Jewish age and the end-time calendar. And the dates and events of that end-time calendar are found to correspond with first century fulfilment of the seventieth week of Daniel's prophecy. Further, Russell's system, without the additions which have yet to be considered, has the appearance of a complete system; it is a logical unity within a larger whole. As such it could be described as a sort of futurism in the course of fulfilment.

Futurist premillennialism properly so called, of course, has little or no interest in current affairs, for they have no bearing upon the understanding of the prophecies. Russell, on the other hand, was deeply interested in world politics for that was the arena in which his theories were to receive their confirmation. He remained, therefore, a thoroughgoing historicist in his approach. However, as had happened in the past, it was to happen again that the expected fulfilments would not materialise. The disappointments of the past had pushed millennialists in two directions: those who persevered with a historicist approach moved out towards the fringes of the Church and beyond; those who stayed close to the Christian mainstream, or tried to do so, distanced themselves from historicism, which had come to appear almost completely discredited, and from world affairs by moving towards a futurist approach to millennialism. By the time of Russell's death and the failure of his system, the Watch Tower movement had migrated well out to the fringe of the Church. As will become apparent in due course, amendments to the system following Russell's death were to carry the process of isolation much further. Those amendments were, perhaps, made the more easy by the 'futurism-in-fulfilment' which has been noted at the core of Russell's system. But unlike futurism proper, which had enabled others to remain within reach of the mainstream whilst distancing themselves from historicism, Watch Tower millennialism led only to increasing isolation. Where Russell had begun to distance his movement from mainstream Protestantism, later Watch Tower revision took further the process of isolation by distancing the movement also from nineteenth-century historicist premillennialism, the tradition within which it had arisen.

Notes

1. C. T. Russell, *The Time is at Hand*, p. 203.
2. *Ibid.*, pp. 209f.
3. *Ibid.*, p. 211.

4. *Ibid.*, p. 212.
5. Above, Chapter 5.
6. Russell, *op. cit.*, p.218.
7. *Ibid.*, p. 218.
8. *Ibid.*, p. 218f. See also: Russell, *op. cit.*, pp. 243ff.
9. Above, Chapter 5.
10. Russell, *op. cit.*, pp. 92f.
11. *Ibid.*, p. 242.
12. *Ibid.*, p. 235.
13. *Ibid.*, p. 240.
14. Above, Chapter 4.

Chapter Seven
Interpreting the Book of Daniel

In the third volume of *Studies in the Scriptures*, *Thy Kingdom Come*, Russell enters familiar ground as he sets out his beliefs concerning the interpretation of the prophecies of Daniel 11 and 12. His approach is that of the historicist premillennialist and much of the detail is the common currency of that tradition. Before proceeding to a detailed examination of Russell's version of the tradition, however, it will be useful to set out the main variations in the interpretation of the apocalyptic passages of Daniel, with particular reference to chapter 11.

There are three broad categories of approach to the interpretation of Daniel 11. The *historical-critical* approach finds in this chapter a useful means by which the casting of Daniel into its latest form can be dated, for the larger part of the chapter comprises a fairly easily decipherable history of middle eastern affairs down to the time of Antiochus Epiphanes (175 BC-164 BC). At verse 40 there is a clear change from the description of what had already taken place to a prediction of events which were expected to mark the end of Antiochus' reign but which never occurred.

Those who adopt the *futurist* approach generally regard the whole of the chapter as prophecy. That the final verses find no reference in the career of Antiochus indicates, not the time when reporting gives way to failed prophecy and, hence, the date when the writing of the book or its latest editing was completed, but rather, that at some point during the course of the chapter the reference has changed. The final verses, then, are to have their fulfilment at some time in the future. The point at which the reference moves from the historical to the future varies with different adherents of this view. Gray, for example, applies verses 21-35 to Antiochus and verse 36 onwards to the events of the end time. [1] Anderson, on the other hand, believed that everything from verse 5 onwards was to have a future fulfilment. [2]

For the *historicist*, the chapter's reference repeatedly moves on, giving an outline of world history until the beginning of the end time, which follows without interval.

World History in Daniel

This section sets out, in broad outline only, the main variations in the interpretation of Daniel 11. Concerning the opening verses there is widespread agreement, but as the chapter proceeds the different approaches to it diverge. Russell, it will be seen, largely follows the Adventist historicist approach exemplified by Uriah Smith, but with some variations. The significance of Russell's variations, however, should be treated with some caution; it is probable that these represent variation within the Adventist tradition rather than any divergence from that tradition for which Russell himself may be responsible.

1. Also I in the first year of Darius the Mede, even I, stood to confirm and to strengthen him.

2. And now I will shew thee the truth. Behold, there shall stand up yet three kings in Persia; and the fourth shall be far richer than they all: and by his strength through his riches he shall stir up all against the realm of Grecia.

3. And a mighty king shall stand up, that shall rule with great dominion, and do according to his will.

4. And when he shall stand up, his kingdom shall be broken, and shall be divided toward the four winds of heaven; and not to his posterity, nor according to his dominion which he ruled: for his kingdom shall be plucked up, even for others beside those.

There are minor variations in the lists given of the four kings referred to in verse 2, but they need not concern us.[3] There appears to be unanimous agreement that the mighty king of verse 3 is Alexander the Great and that verse 4 refers to the division of his empire by his four generals following his death.[4] Cassander ruled the western part of the empire; Seleucus ruled the eastern part; Lysimachus ruled the northern territories which comprised Thrace and Asia Minor; and Ptolemy ruled Egypt, the southern territory.

5. And the king of the south shall be strong, and one of his princes; and he shall be strong above him, and have dominion; his dominion shall be a great dominion.

6. And in the end of years they shall join themselves together; for the king's daughter of the south shall come to the king of the north to make an agreement: but she shall not retain the power of the arm; neither shall he stand, nor his arm: but she shall be given up, and they that brought her, and he that begat her, and he that strengthened her in these times.

Verse 6 refers to an agreement between Ptolemy II Philadelphus of Egypt (the king of the south) and Antiochus III Theos of Syria (the king of the north) which required Antiochus to divorce his wife Laodice and marry Berenice, daughter of Ptolemy. Berenice, however, did not retain the power, for Antiochus restored Laodice to the royal court and she, fearing further deposition, had both Berenice and Antiochus murdered.[5]

7. But out of a branch of her roots shall one stand up in his estate, which shall come with an army, and shall enter into the fortress of the king of the north, and shall deal against them, and shall prevail:

The branch here referred to is Berenice's brother, Ptolemy Euergetes, who succeeded his father, Ptolemy Philadelphus, and raised an army to avenge the death of his sister.[6]

8. And shall also carry captives into Egypt their gods, with their princes,

and with their precious vessels of silver and of gold; and he shall
continue more years than the king of the north.

9. So the king of the south shall come into his kingdom, and shall
return into his own land.

10. But his sons shall be stirred up, and shall assemble a multitude of
great forces: and one shall certainly come, and overflow, and pass
through: then shall he return, and be stirred up, even to his fortress.

The sons here mentioned are Seleucus Ceraunus and Antiochus Magnus.
Seleucus first took the throne but was murdered, whereupon Antiochus became
king. He reconquered Seleucia and recovered Syria.[7]

11. And the king of the south shall be moved with choler, and shall
come forth and fight with him, even with the king of the north: and he
shall set forth a great multitude; but the multitude shall be given into
his hand.

Ptolemy Philopater succeeded his father Euergetes and defeated Antiochus
Magnus in battle.[8]

12. And when he hath taken away the multitude, his heart shall be
lifted up; and he shall cast down many ten thousands: but he shall not
be strengthened by it.

13. For the king of the north shall return, and shall set forth a multitude
greater than the former, and shall certainly come after certain years
with a great army and with much riches.

Ptolemy Philopater, however, failed to make good his victory and was
reconquered by Antiochus Magnus. Subsequently there was peace between
the two powers for fourteen years. Ptolemy was succeeded by Ptolemy
Epiphanes, who was still only a child when he came to the throne. Antiochus
set out against Egypt expecting an easy victory over the young king.[9]

14. And in those times there shall many stand up against the king of
the south: also the robbers of thy people shall exalt themselves to
establish the vision; but they shall fall.

Egypt now came under attack from all around. Those provinces which had
hitherto been subject to Egypt rebelled. Philip of Macedon and Antiochus
joined forces with the intention of dividing Ptolemy's territories between
them. At this point the newly emerging Roman empire comes into the
reckoning, identified by the prophecy, according to Smith, as 'the robbers of
thy people'.[10] Porteous, however, applies this phrase to Jews who sided with
Antiochus.[11] The Romans intervened on behalf of the young Egyptian king in
order to defeat the alliance between Philip and Antiochus.[12] Smith believed
that the significance of this first interference in the affairs of the kings of the
north and south by Rome was indicated in the prophecy by the words 'to
establish the vision'. That is, the Roman Empire is to figure more prominently
than any other in Daniel's prophecy; its emergence now demonstrates the
truth of the vision in which the existence of such a power had been
prophesied.[13] Porteous prefers to conclude that the meaning of the words 'to
establish the vision' is not clearly understood, rather than that the fulfilment
of a prediciton is thereby indicated.[14] The words 'they shall fall' had an
immediate fulfilment if they refer to the those who attacked Egypt at the time
of Ptolemy Epiphanes. On the other hand, if the reference is to Rome, then
the fulfilment is in the distant future.[15]

15. So the king of the north shall come, and cast up a mount, and take the most fenced cities: and the arms of the south shall not withstand, neither his chosen people, neither shall there be any strength to withstand.

16. But he that comest against him shall do according to his own will, and none shall stand before him: and he shall stand in the glorious land, which by his hand shall be consumed.

Egypt proved unable to withstand the attack of Antiochus but he, in turn, was unable to withstand Rome. Verse 16 reaches the point at which the Roman Empire extended its territories to include Judaea, 'the glorious land'.[16]

17. He shall also set his face to enter with the strength of his whole kingdom, and upright ones with him; thus shall he do: and he shall give him the daughter of women, corrupting her: but she shall not stand on his side, neither be for him.

With verse 17 the point is reached where Rome finally consolidated its hold of Egypt. Ptolemy, the son of Ptolemy Auletes, and his sister Cleopatra succeeded to the throne but because they were too young to exercise authority they were placed under the guardianship of the Romans. Pompey was their first guardian but, following his murder, Caesar Augustus assumed the guardianship. He demanded that Ptolemy and Cleopatra should disband their armies and the outcome of the ensuing tension was that Rome absorbed Egypt into its empire.

Russell gives scant detail of the application of the prophecy up to this point. 'Since all are agreed thus far, we need go no farther into the past.' [17] From about this point onwards, however, the broad agreement between the different traditions of interpretation ceases. The historical-critical approach and that of some futurist interpreters continue to apply the prophecy to the struggles between the Syrian and Egyptian kingdoms as far as the reign of Antiochus Epiphanes. Russell, largely following the traditional historicist approach, on the other hand, sets out in a different direction.

18. After this shall he turn his face to the isles, and shall take many: but a prince for his own behalf shall cause the reproach offered by him to cease; wi thout his own reproach he shall cause it to turn upon him.

19. Then he shall turn his face toward the fort of his own land: but he shall stumble and fall, and not be found.

20. Then shall stand up in his estate a raiser of taxes in the glory of the kingdom: but within a few days he shall be destroyed, neither in anger, nor in battle.

The historical-critical and most futurist approaches apply verse 20 to Seleucus IV, who was noted as a raiser of taxes. For the historicist, the reference is to Caesar Augustus, who was especially noted in Scripture in this regard: 'There went out a decree from Caesar Augustus, that all the world should be taxed' (Luke 2:1). [18]

21. And in his estate shall stand up a vile person, to whom they shall not give the honour of the kingdom: but he shall come in peaceably, and obtain the kingdom by flatteries.

22. And with the arms of a flood shall they be overflown from before

him, and shall be broken; yea, also the prince of the covenant.

Caesar Augustus was followed by Tiberius Caesar, the 'vile person' whose reign was marked by cruelty and slaughter. The worst of the crimes of that period, of course, was the murder of the 'prince of the covenant', the crucifixion of Jesus. [19]

23. And after the league made with him he shall come deceitfully: for
he shall come up, and shall become strong with a small people.

Having introduced Rome into the picture with a glimpse of the state of affairs around the time of Jesus, the Adventist interpretation of the prophecy then reverts to an earlier period to describe the beginnings and the growth of Roman influence. The league referred to in verse 23, then, is the league between the Jews and Rome of 161 BC. The Jewish people, suffering from oppression by the Syrians, sought assistance from the Romans who were, at that time, a relatively insignificant nation. What Rome lacked in force, she made up for by stealth, hence the reference to coming deceitfully.[20]

Russell continues to apply the prophecy to Tiberius: the league referred to here is the Senate's recognition of Tiberius as emperor and the 'small people' with whom he became strong represent the Praetorian Guard which he organised. [21]

24. He shall enter peaceably even upon the fattest places of the
province; and he shall do that which his fathers have not done, nor his
fathers' fathers; he shall scatter among them the prey, and spoil, and
riches: yea, and he shall forecast his devices against the strong holds,
even for a time.

Verse 24 describes a new departure in international affairs. Whereas rulers had, until this time, sought to extend their territories only by warfare, Rome began a different policy and the Roman Empire expanded peaceably as states came willingly under Rome for the protection which she afforded.

For Russell, the policy of peaceable dealings with neighbours and provinces was more strongly established during the time of Augustus and his successors than before. [22]

25. And he shall stir up his power and his courage against the king of
the south with a great army; and the king of the south shall be stirred
up to battle with a very great and mighty army; but he shall not stand:
for they shall forecast devices against him.

26. Yea, they that feed of the portion of his meat shall destroy him,
and his army shall overflow: and many shall fall down slain.

Not all of Rome's dealings with other states, of course, were peaceable. Verse 25, according to the Adventist interpretation, describes the battle of Actium in 31 BC between Rome and Egypt, when Antony was defeated. The cause of Antony's downfall was the desertion of his allies – 'they that feed of the portion of his meat'. [23]

Russell applies the battle of verse 25 to Aurelian's attack upon Queen Zenobia of Egypt in AD 272. [24] However, events are out of sequence in this interpretation, for verse 26 is applied to Aurelian's assassination by his own generals, whereas verse 28 is applied to his return from Egypt after the defeat of Zenobia.[25]

27. And both these kings' hearts shall be to do mischief, and they shall speak lies at one table; but it shall not prosper: for the end shall be at the time appointed.

28. Then shall he return into his land with great riches; and his heart shall be against the holy covenant; and he shall do exploits, and return to his own land.

Smith applies these verses to two Roman campaigns: verse 27 indicates the mutual deception between Octavian and Antony and the first part of the following verse refers to Octavian's return following his successful expedition against Antony; the second return mentioned in verse 28 refers to the conclusion of the campaign against Judaea, which included the destruction of Jerusalem in AD 70. [26]

For Russell, verse 28 refers to Aurelian's return with honour to Rome following his suppression of Zenobia. The two kings of the previous verse are not the respective political rulers but rather two powers within the Roman Empire. They are the imperial power which is now gradually dying and the ecclesiastical power which is slowly rising. For Russell, the expression 'the time appointed' or its equivalent in prophecy refers, not to any set time but, specifically, to the 'time of the end'. So, the final clause of the verse, 'the end shall be at the time appointed', indicates that the ecclesiastical power, the power of the papacy, will extend until the 'time of the end'.[27]

29. At the time appointed he shall return, and come toward the south; but it shall not be as the former, or as the latter.

30. For the ships of Chittim shall come against him: therefore he shall be grieved, and return, and have indignation against the holy covenant: so shall he do; he shall even return, and have intelligence with them that forsake the holy covenant.

Again, the expression 'at the time appointed' indicates to Russell that verses 29 and 30 are a parenthesis looking forward to the major conflict between the imperial and ecclesiastical powers at the 'time of the end'. [28]

According to Smith, verse 30 refers to the attack upon Rome from Carthage by the Vandals under Genseric. 'Intelligence with them that forsake the holy covenant' is a reference to the Roman state's connivance with the apostate Church of Rome which, following the defeat of the Arian Goths, resulted in papal supremacy. [29]

31. And arms shall stand on his part and they shall pollute the sanctuary of strength, and shall take away the daily sacrifice, and they shall place the abomination that maketh desolate.

At this point Russell's and Smith's interpretations begin to converge. Both are agreed that 'the abomination that maketh desolate' is the papacy. Smith, however, believed that the removal of the daily sacrifice indicated the supplanting of Roman paganism by Roman Catholicism,[30] but Russell, preferring the rendering, 'continual sacrifice', believed that the prophecy referred to Jesus' continual, or once-for-all, sacrificial death. The removal of the continual sacrifice, then, was achieved when the true meaning of Jesus' sacrifice was supplanted by the apostate doctrines of transubstantiation and the sacrifice of the mass. [31]

It is necessary here to resume consideration of the historical-critical and futurist approaches, for the historical events which they consider to be indicated by the prophecy are now nearing their climax. In this interpretation verse 31 refers to the desecration of the Temple by Antiochus Epiphanes when he erected a pagan altar there and put an end, for a time, to Jewish sacrificial worship. [32]

32. And such as do wickedly against the covenant shall he corrupt by flatteries: but the people that do know their God shall be strong, and do exploits.

33. And they that understand among the people shall instruct many: yet they shall fall by the sword, and by flame, by captivity, and by spoil, many days.

34. Now when they shall fall, they shall be holpen with a little help: but many shall cleave to them with flatteries.

35. And some of them of understanding shall fall, to try them, and to purge, and to make them white, even to the time of the end: because it is yet for a time appointed.

In the historicist interpretation, which is followed by both Smith and Russell, these verses refer to the continuing conflict between the papacy and the true Church. Verse 34 is a reference to the Protestant Reformation and to the fact that many embraced the Protestant cause from unworthy motives. [33]

The historical-critical approach and that of most futurists apply these verses to the struggles between faithful Jews and the armies of Antiochus. Verse 34 refers to the successful uprising under Judas Maccabaeus.

At this point the historical-critical approach, finding no further events in the career of Antiochus which correspond with the remaining verses of the chapter, identifies the transition from reporting to prediction. Futurist interpreters, likewise, acknowledge that Antiochus' affairs cease to be depicted after verse 35 but they apply the rest of the chapter to the yet future end time when they will have their fulfilment in Antichrist. [34]

36. And the king shall do according to his will; and he shall magnify himself above every god, and shall speak marvellous things against the God of gods, and shall prosper till the indignation be accomplished: for that that is determined shall be done.

At verse 36 the prophecy, according to both Smith and Russell, begins to outline the major events which mark the onset of the 'time of the end'. Both see the prophecy's fulfilment in France, but where Smith identifies the king with the government of France at the time of the Revolution and thereafter,[35] Russell believes that Napoleon is indicated individually.[36] Some minor variations follow from this difference of application but nothing of major significance seems to be involved. In what follows only Russell's interpretation is given.

It should be noted that in verse 36 the word 'god' is being used in the sense of 'mighty one' or 'ruler' and not necessarily as indicating divinity, though Napoleon was noteworthy as the first major political leader to acknowledge no deity. His ambition was to exalt himself above all other rulers. Especially important is his opposition to the 'god of gods' – by which, again, no deity is meant; rather, this indicates Napoleon's opposition to the 'ruler of rulers', which Russell understood as indicating the papacy. [37]

37. Neither shall he regard the God of his fathers, nor the desire of

women, nor regard any god: for he shall magnify himself above all.

Napoleon rejected both Roman Catholicism, the 'God of his fathers,' and Protestantism, 'the desire of women'.[38]

38. But in his estate shall he honour the God of forces: and a god whom his fathers knew not shall he honour with gold, and silver, and with precious stones, and pleasant things.

For Napoleon the only God was, in effect, military strength; and where all military leaders before him had invariably ascribed their victories to their gods, Napoleon ascribed his success to his own genius, a 'god whom his fathers knew not'.[39]

39. Thus shall he do in the most strong holds with a strange god, whom he shall acknowledge and increase with glory: and he shall cause them to rule over many, and shall divide the land for gain.

40. And at the time of the end shall the king of the south push at him: and the king of the north shall come against him like a whirlwind, with chariots, and with horsemen, and with many ships; and he shall enter into the countries, and shall overflow and pass over.

It was noted above that, in Russell's system, verses 29 and 30 were regarded as parenthetical, referring to a major conflict which was to mark the 'time of the end'. That conflict is now described, beginning at verse 40. It is Napoleon's invasion of Egypt between May 1798 and October 1799. During that campaign he fought against the king of the south, that is, against Egypt, and was attacked by the king of the north which, by this time, signified England. [40]

41. He shall enter also into the glorious land, and many countries shall be overthrown: but these shall escape out of his hand, even Edom, and Moab, and the chief of the children of Ammon.

42. He shall stretch forth his hand also upon the countries: and the land of Egypt shall not escape.

43. But he shall have power over the treasures of gold and of silver, and over all the precious things of Egypt: and the Libyans and the Ethiopians shall be at his steps.

44. But tidings out of the east and out of the north shall trouble him: therefore he shall go forth with great fury to destroy, and utterly to make away many.

45. And he shall plant the tabernacles of his palace between the seas in the glorious holy mountain; yet he shall come to his end, and none shall help him.

The final verses of the chapter describe the progress of Napoleon's Egyptian campaign until developments in Europe compelled him to return to France (verse 44). His attempted suppression of the European nations led to his defeat and exile, forsaken by all. [41]

The most significant outcome of Napoleon's career was the effective end of papal influence over European political affairs. Although Napoleon did eventually enter into an agreement with Pope Pius VII, the Concordat of 1801, whereby the Roman Catholic religion was re-established in France, the old stranglehold could never again be restored.

Napoleon's work, together with the French Revolution, broke the spell of religious superstition, humbled the pride of self-exalted religious lords, awakened the world to a fuller sense of the powers and prerogatives of manhood and broke the Papal dominion against which the religious Reformation had previously struck a death blow, but which its after course had healed. (Rev. 13:3) The era closing with A.D. 1799, marked by Napoleon's Egyptian campaign, sealed and defined the limit of Papal dominion over the nations. [42]

That date also marked the beginning of a new era characterised by liberty of thought, by increasing political freedom both in Europe and in America, and by growth in Bible publishing. [43]

Observations

Before proceeding to an examination of Russell's further expectations for the 'time of the end', it is worthwhile to pause to consider the implications of the foregoing for our view of the use of the Bible in religious discourse. It is all too easy to dismiss systems of interpretation such as Russell's as having more in common with the interpretation of Nostradamus and Mother Shipton than with biblical exegesis. Once it is observed that most of the predictions generated by such systems have failed, it seems reasonable to suppose that the study of those systems can yield little of any value. This attitude is, I believe, mistaken.

It is entirely natural, of course, that the past failures and embarrassments of historicist premillennialism should predispose most modern readers in favour of a view of Daniel similar to that of the historical-critical scholar. The arguments concerning the date when Daniel was written are persuasive. If those arguments are accepted, then it seems that there can be little room left for genuine prophecy, at any rate of the sort which may be interpreted along historicist lines. And if that is the case, then Daniel can or, indeed, must be treated as a work of pious fiction aimed at boosting the morale of the Jewish people during one of the more difficult periods of their history. As such, its continuing relevance may seem limited. It is an outstanding example of a particular literary genre which may be valued by later generations in much the same way that other truly great literary works are valued. If that is how Daniel is to be regarded then, in my view, it certainly does deserve a prominent place within the corpus of literature of the Judaeo-Christian tradition. Such a view, however, raises some questions which ought not to be ignored.

The first question to consider is whether it is possible to hold a historical-critical view of Daniel without that having implications for how other parts of Scripture are to be regarded. That Daniel was regarded from an early stage as genuinely what it purports to be seems fairly certain, for it must be highly improbable that it should have been treated as sacred Scripture and eventually included in both the Jewish and the Christian canons if it was believed to have been a late composition all of whose attempts at prophecy had failed. But if that is the case, then it is also highly probable that those sections now regarded as failed predictions about Antiochus Epiphanes would have been understood as prophecies about something else. Indeed, Josephus reflects the belief that the visions of Daniel foretold events both at the time of Antiochus Epiphanes and during the first century AD. [44]

If, as was argued in Chapter 2, Daniel has provided the background for much important New Testament thinking, then it seems certain that the belief was prevalent among the earliest Christians that Daniel contained prophecy then awaiting fulfilment. More importantly, any view of Daniel must have its counterpart in our view of those New Testament passages which draw directly upon Daniel. A position at either of two extremes may be held with consistency: thoroughgoing scepticism with respect to the whole of Scripture can be consistent; and a traditionalist position can also be consistent. That is not to imply that either position must be correct, only that either may be held without self-contradiction. But the middle ground may be more difficult to occupy. A traditionalist view of the New Testament together with a historical-critical view of Daniel has an apparent self-contradiction to be resolved, for if New Testament teaching does draw upon Daniel then some sort of traditionalist view of Daniel seems also to be implied.

For the purposes of the present study, the main implication from the foregoing concerns the foundations upon which the historicist approach to Daniel is constructed. Though writers in the tradition have undoubtedly been led astray by their enthusiasm for the application of prophecy to current and historical affairs, it is an oversimplification to suggest that their enterprise rests wholly upon a misuse of Scripture. Whilst acknowledging the persuasiveness of the historical-critical view, the historicist (and the futurist) position can be presented as the claim that the application of Daniel to the second century BC does not exhaust its meaning and that its application to events yet future is implied in the Gospels. That being so, the failure of any particular application of the prophecies will not necessarily undermine perseverance in the tradition.

Notes

1. James M. Gray, *Commentary on the Whole Bible*, p. 361.
2. Sir Robert Anderson, *The Coming Prince*, p. 195.
3. Norman Porteous, *Daniel: A Commentary*, p. 158.
4. *Ibid.*, p. 159.
5. *Ibid.*, p. 160.
6. *Ibid.*, p. 160.
7. *Ibid.*, p. 161.
8. *Ibid.*, p. 162.
9. *Ibid.*, p. 162.
10. Uriah Smith, *Daniel and the Revelation*, p. 229.
11. Porteous, *op. cit.*, p. 163.
12. *Ibid.*, p. 164.
13. Smith, *op. cit.*, p. 231.
14. Porteous, *op. cit.*, p. 163.
15. Smith, *op. cit.*, p. 231.
16. Porteous, *op. cit.*, pp. 163f.
17. C. T. Russell, *Thy Kingdom Come*, p. 28.
18. *Ibid.*, p. 29. Smith, *op. cit.*, p. 237.

19.C. T. Russell, *Thy Kingdom Come*, p. 30. U. Smith, *Daniel and the Revelation*, p. 240.

20.*Ibid.*, p. 241.

21.Russell, *op. cit.*, p. 30.

22.*Ibid.*, p. 31.

23.Smith, *op. cit.*, p. 242.

24.Russell, *op. cit.*, p. 33.

25.*Ibid.*, p. 33.

26.Smith, *op. cit.*, p. 247.

27.Russell, *op. cit.*, pp. 34f.

28.*Ibid.*, p. 35

29.Smith, *op. cit.*, pp. 249f.

30.*Ibid.*, p. 251.

31.Russell, *op. cit.*, pp. 35ff.

32.Porteous, *op. cit.*, p. 168.

33.Smith, *op. cit.*, p. 258. Russell, *op. cit.*, p. 38.

34.Gray, *op. cit.*, p. 360.

35.Smith, *op. cit.*, pp. 259f.

36.Russell, *op. cit.*, p. 40.

37.*Ibid.*, p. 40.

38.*Ibid.*, p. 42.

39.*Ibid.*, p. 43.

40.*Ibid.*, pp. 44f.

41.*Ibid.*, p. 46.

42.*Ibid.*, p. 50.

43.*Ibid.*, pp. 50f.

44.Josephus, *Antiquities*, 10.10.4.

Chapter Eight
Days of Waiting

By his exposition of Daniel 11, Russell identified AD 1799 as the year when the 'time of the end' was due to begin. His approach as far as this point is, to all intents and purposes, an Adventist approach with minor variations. However, just as his use of the Jubilee cycle and the 'Plan of the Ages' was distinctive and innovative, so his interpretation of Daniel 12 represents a new departure in historicist premillennialism. Briefly, the significant difference between Miller's and Russell's interpretations of the periods of days referred to in Daniel 12, is that where Miller had found different starting points for each and had terminated the three periods at only two points, AD 1798 and AD 1843, Russell takes the same starting point for each and, hence, identifies three different termini.

The Time of the End – Daniel 12
1. And at that time shall Michael stand up, the great prince which standeth for the children of thy people: and there shall be a time of trouble, such as never was since there was a nation even to that same time: and at that time thy people shall be delivered, every one that shall be found written in the book.
2. And many of them that sleep in the dust of the earth shall awake, some to everlasting life, and some to shame and everlasting contempt.
3. And they that be wise shall shine as the brightness of the firmament; and they that turn many to righteousness as the stars for ever and ever.
In these three verses the grand outcome of God's plan is described. For the expression 'at that time' Russell prefers 'in that time' the point being that Michael's standing up should not be understood as happening at the point just identified, namely, AD 1799. Rather, Michael is due to stand up, or take power, at some time during the 'time of the end', the period which began in AD 1799. The name Michael means 'Who is like God', and therefore signifies one who represents God; it is used here to represent Christ, the Messiah, who, at the appointed time, will deliver the people of God from sin, ignorance, pain and death, and from all the troubles which the agents of Satan have brought against them.

As verse 1 indicates, the Millennium will be inaugurated by a time of trouble throughout the world, in comparison with which all previous wars and revolutions will pale into insignificance.

During the Millennium all those who in past ages have been found worthy will be resurrected, though, as verse 3 indicates, some are singled out for special honour. These are the ones whom Russell styles 'overcomers', who include especially the patriarchs, the prophets, and outstanding men of faith of the Jewish and Patriarchal ages.

With this brief description of the Millennium and events leading up to it, the prophecy comes to an end. What follows provides certain clues whereby it is possible for the reader to become convinced, in God's due time, that the prophecy has become due for fulfilment.[1]

4. But thou, O Daniel, shut up the words and seal the book, even to the time of the end: many shall run to and fro, and knowledge shall be increased.

5. Then I Daniel looked, and, behold, there stood other two, the one on this side of the bank of the river, and the other on that side of the bank of the river.

6. And one said to the man clothed in linen, which was upon the waters of the river, How long shall it be to the end of these wonders?

7. And I heard the man clothed in linen, which was upon the waters of the river, when he held up his right hand and his left hand unto heaven, and sware by him that liveth for ever that it shall be for a time, times, and an half; and when he shall have accomplished to scatter the power of the holy people, all these things shall be finished.

8. And I heard, but I understood not: then said I, O my Lord, what shall be the end of these things?

9. And he said, Go thy way, Daniel: for the words are closed up and sealed till the time of the end.

The meaning of Daniel's prophecies remained hidden until the 'time of the end'. Though many have attempted to explain the book, they have been unable to do so to any satisfactory extent because it was not God's will that the meaning should become apparent until some time during the 'time of the end'.

Daniel is told that the vision will begin to have its fulfilment after 'a time, and times, and an half'. Following Miller, Russell adopted the traditional explanation of this expression. It is three-and-a-half times or years and is the same period referred to at Daniel 7:25 and Revelation 12:6,14; 13:5. From those scriptures it is apparent that three-and-a-half years is equivalent to forty-two months or 1,260 days. Following the year-for-a-day principle, then, this indicates a total period of 1,260 years which is the extent of the period of the papacy's power. Linking this with what was learned in the previous chapter, namely, that papal power extended to AD 1799 when it was brought to an end by Napoleon, it is possible to determine that it began in AD 539. Though Russell had arrived at this date by counting back from AD 1799 on the basis of his understanding of the 1,260 days, history, he believed, confirmed his theory. He did not, however, believe that it would have been possible to identify this beginning of papal power by purely historical study without first having understood the meaning of the 1,260 days. Given that understanding, the significance of AD 539 becomes apparent.[2] Having established this date, it then becomes possible to interpret the remaining periods mentioned in the prophecy.

10. Many shall be purified, and made white, and tried; but the wicked shall

do wickedly: and none of the wicked shall understand; but the wise shall understand.

11. And from the time that the daily sacrifice shall be taken away, and the abomination that maketh desolate set up, there shall be a thousand two hundred and ninety days.

12. Blessed is he that waiteth, and cometh to the thousand three hundred and five and thirty days.

13. But go thy way till the end be: for thou shalt rest, and stand in thy lot at the end of the days.

Miller, as was noted above, had understood the taking away of the daily sacrifice as the end of Roman paganism in AD 508 and took that as the beginning of the 1,290 years indicated in verse 11 which, therefore, he terminated at the same point as the 1,260 years.[3] For Russell, however, the taking away of the daily (or continual) sacrifice and the setting up of the 'abomination that maketh desolate', though they are separate events, are part of a process whereby the abomination supplants the sacrifice. Consequently, there is no room for a different starting point for the 1,290 years in Russell's system, for both periods must count from when the process of setting up the abomination is complete. The 1,290 years, then, begin in AD 539 and extend to AD 1829, thirty years after the beginning of the 'time of the end'. The 1,335 years indicated in verse 12, likewise, must have the same starting point and therefore extend to AD 1874.[4]

Modern historical-critical scholarship generally regards these two periods which have been introduced near the end of chapter 12 as evidence of later editing.[5] Anticipated events at the close of the three-and-a-half years not having transpired, an editor probably sought to extend the period to 1,290 days. Likewise, when the 1,290 days passed without the prophecy's fulfilment, a further editor extended the period to 1,335 days. It is for this reason that both these periods appear to be lacking any stated *terminus a quo* or *terminus ad quem*. The *termini* have already been stated in connection with the three-and-a-half years.

Modern scholarship, however, generally assumes that Daniel 12:4 offers an explanation for the first appearance during the second century BC of a prophecy (not necessarily the entire book) purportedly given during the exile. The prophecy's circulation, or being made public, constitutes its unsealing. To Russell and those of related traditions, however, the original appearance of Daniel in its final form during the sixth century BC was never equated with its unsealing. From its first being written until the 'time of the end', Daniel remained a sealed book. Given this assumption, the *terminus ad quem* of the 1,290 days is plainly obvious; it is stated in the immediately preceding verses:

> And he said, Go thy way, Daniel: for the words are closed up and sealed till the time of the end. Many shall be purified, and made white, and tried; but the wicked shall do wickedly: and none of the wicked shall understand; but the wise shall understand. (Daniel 12:9,10)

The expiry of the 1,290 days in 1829, then, marks the time when the prophecies of Daniel begin at last to be understood. So, for Russell, the Adventist movement was of considerable importance:

It was the beginning of the right understanding of Daniel's visions, and at the right time to fit the prophecy. Mr. Miller's application of the three and a half times (1260 years) was practically the same as that we have just given. . . . Mr. Miller was an earnest and esteemed member of the Baptist Church; and, being a careful student of the Scriptures, the prophecies began to open before him. . . . The beginning of this work among the Baptist ministers was, as nearly as can be learned from his memoirs, in 1829. . . . Thus it will be seen that the separating work of the 'Miller movement' had its beginning at the time foretold,– at the end of the 1290 days, 1829.[6]

The *terminus ad quem* of the 1,335 days is described only indirectly. The prophecy makes no mention, at this point, of the events which are to transpire at the close the 1,335 days but only of the condition at that time of the faithful:

Blessed is he that waiteth, and cometh to the thousand three hundred and five and thirty days. (Daniel 12:12)

The end of this period, then, is to be marked by a state of especial blessedness following a time of waiting.

Who have thus waited? Some of God's children, the 'holy people,' the writer among the number, though not associated with the 'Miller movement,' nor with the denomination subsequently organized, which calls itself the 'Second Advent Church,' have been looking and 'earnestly waiting' for Michael's Kingdom; and gladly we bear testimony to the 'blessedness' of the wonderfully clear unfoldings of our Father's plan, at and since the fall of 1874 – the end of the 1335 days.[7]

With this interpretation of Daniel 12:12, Russell incorporated into his system a development of the explanation, which had become current among continuing Adventists, for the disappointment of 1844. For Russell, as for Adventists before him, the parable of the wise and foolish virgins (Matthew 25:1-13) is a forewarning in Scripture that at the time of Christ's second presence there will be a time of waiting which will test the faithfulness of many. But in Russell's system the end of the period of waiting for the Bridegroom is clearly identified:

Disappointment was predicted for the first movement, and waiting for the 1335 days was necessary; but the second was not a disappointment, and a waiting was no longer necessary; for fulfilment came exactly at the close of the 1335 prophetic days – in October 1874. It was just following the close of the 1335 years, the period of 'waiting,' that the fact of our Lord's presence, as taught by the foregoing prophecies, began to be recognized.[8]

Russell's acknowledgement of Miller's importance in the development of Millennialism has already been mentioned.[9] His interpretation of the significance of the 1,290 days and the 1,335 days, it should be noted, goes much further than this acknowledgement; it provides, within Russell's own system, a theological description of Miller's role. Russell's ecclesiology, if such it can be styled, then, encompasses the movement which began with Miller. The importance of this will become apparent later when considering the ecclesiology of the Watch Tower movement under the presidency of Joseph Rutherford and afterwards.

Cleansing the Sanctuary

There remains one prophecy to be dealt with and then the setting out of Russell's end-time calendar will be complete. This is the prophecy of the 2,300 days which, it was noted earlier,[10] began to engage the attention of millennialists once the application of the 1,260 days to the period ending with the French Revolution had gained widespread acceptance.

> How long shall be the vision concerning the daily sacrifice, and the transgression of desolation, to give both the sanctuary and the host to be trodden underfoot? And he said unto me, Unto two thousand and three hundred days; then shall the sanctuary be cleansed. (Daniel 8:13,14)

Modern scholarship is generally agreed that the expression here rendered 'days' is better rendered 'evenings and mornings'. The daily sacrifices to which the prophecy refers, involved both evening and morning sacrifice, and the reference is to 2,300 such sacrifices. The period indicated, then, is 1,150 days rather than 2,300 days.[11] Given this understanding of the prophecy, it can be recognised that what is found in chapter 12 is a reiteration of what was given in chapter 8. The three-and-a-half years of chapter 12, then, is simply an alternative designation of the same period referred to in chapter 8 as 2,300 evenings and mornings.

This explanation of the prophecy, persuasive though it may be to the modern reader, is unlikely to hold much appeal for the historicist mind. Like the historical-critical application of the seventy weeks which was noted earlier,[12] this interpretation implies a lack of concern with precision which does not commend itself to the historicist. Indeed, such numerical looseness sits oddly with the concern for precision implied by the interpretation of the 1,290 days and 1,335 days as later editorial glosses aimed at matching the predictions to developing affairs. The historicist sees this concern for precision throughout the prophecies and, so long as it is possible to offer interpretations which seem to preserve such numerical accuracy, the views of modern scholarship will carry little weight.

Russell, following the tradition, understands the period indicated by Daniel 8:14 as 2,300 prophetic years. Like Miller, he argues that the prophecy of the seventy weeks in the following chapter indicates the start of the longer period:

> As these seventy weeks, or 490 days, were the forepart of the 2300, their fulfilment not only serves to show us when the 2300 began, but also to show what manner of time (literal or symbolic) was signified.[13]

The 2,300 years begin to count, then, from the same time that the 490 years begin, namely, the decree to rebuild Jerusalem. Interestingly, however, Russell makes no specific mention of the starting point of this period; instead he counts 2,300 years minus 490 years from AD 36, the point at which the seventy weeks terminated, and arrives at 1846.[14] This is the time when the cleansing of the sanctuary may be expected to be complete.

It is important to take note of the distinction which Russell makes between the 'host' and the 'sanctuary', for it is only the latter which is cleansed at the expiry of the 2,300 days.

> The Sanctuary was defiled by the bringing in of various errors with their corresponding evil tendencies, that the climax of these was reached in the introduction of the Mass, and that following in the wake

of this error came the deepest degradation of *the host* (the masses of the church nominal), culminating in the shameless sale of 'indulgences,' which measurably provoked the reform movement. Though the *Sanctuary* class, too, was in a measure defiled, i.e., deceived into this error, the dreadful results opened their eyes to it. And, accordingly, we find that the key-note of the Great Reformation was, Justification by faith in the '*continual sacrifice*' of Christ that needs no repetition. . . . Yet, notice, the prophecy does not indicate a cleansing of the *host* at the time, but of the *Sanctuary* class only. Nor was the host cleansed. They still retained the error, and do to this day; but the consecrated class, the Sanctuary, renounced the error and suffered for the truth's sake, many of them even unto death.[15]

To Russell's recognition of Miller's part in the Divine plan, then, there is added some recognition of elements of the Reformation as the start of the process which was to have its culmination in the emergence in 1846 of the group which was subsequently to lead to the formation of the Watch Tower movement.

Thus AD 1846, the end of the 2,300 days, as shown above, found an unorganised nucleus of Christians, who not only agreed with the 'Disciples' regarding simplicity of church government, the discarding of all creeds but the Bible, and the abolition of all titles by its ministers, but with the 'Baptists' relative to the outward form of baptism, and with Luther in regarding the Papal system as the Man of Sin, and the degenerate church as the mother of harlots and abominations. These, standing aloof from any compromise or affinity with the world, taught vital piety, simple trust in the omnipotent God and faith in his unchangeable decrees; and, in addition, while recognizing Christ as Lord of all, and now partaker of the divine nature, they were guarded against the unscriptural as well as the unreasonable theory that Jehovah is his own Son and our Lord Jesus is his own Father [Russell's characterisation of trinitarian theology]; and they began to see that eternal life and immortality are not present possessions, but are to be expected only as the gifts of God through Christ in the resurrection.[16]

The Work of Harvest

With the cleansing of the Sanctuary, the stage is set for the beginning of a closely-related work which characterises the period of transition from the Gospel age to the Millennial age, namely, the Harvest. This is the point which was reached earlier following the consideration of parallel dispensations[17] but now it becomes possible to add some important detail to the way in which the progress of the true Church over the closing centuries of the Gospel age is understood.

First, it is important to understand that the recognition which Russell accorded to Miller's part in the Divine plan differs in kind from that which he accorded to the Reformation. The difference can be characterised by the relationship between the respective renewal movements and nominal Christianity, and by the nature of the divine involvement with those movements. So the Reformation was, as the word indicates, an attempt to *reform* apostate Christianity, or Babylon the Great, whereas Miller's movement led to the *separation* of the Sanctuary class from Babylon. It is the distinction alluded to in the parable of the wheat and the tares, which are allowed to grow together until the time of the harvest when, at last, they are separated (Matthew 13:24-30). Corresponding with this difference of relationship to Babylon is a difference in the way in which the divine involvement is understood. In the case of the reformers, divine involvement is seen as merely permissive, whereas during the 'time of the end' it becomes directive. That is, the initiative of the reformers received God's blessing but had only limited success because it was not yet the time for the separation between nominal and true Christians. Once that time is reached, however, the separation proceeds in response to the divine initiative.

The parable of the wheat and the tares, then, is a prophetic picture of the separation which must take place during the 'time of the end' between the true Church and the nominal Church. This separation, however, is not to be equated with the cleansing of the Sanctuary which, it has been observed, was completed in 1846. The separating of the wheat and the tares is specifically the work of the Harvest period and occupies the forty years from 1874 to 1914.[18] There may seem, on the face of it, to be some confusion here, for, given that the distinction noted above between attempted reform and separation from Babylon is a crucial factor in the definition of the cleansing of the Sanctuary, it may appear that there is no further distinction to be made which might mark off the next stage in the process, the Harvest of the true Church. Indeed, the Harvest continues the very same process which constituted the cleansing of the Sanctuary. How, then, can it be correct to say that the Harvest does not begin until twenty-eight years after the cleansing of the Sanctuary?

The answer to this question, though Russell does not actually address it as such, becomes apparent with the exposition of the second of the parables which describe the Harvest. This is the parable of the drag-net (Matthew 13:47-50) which describes the same work of separation as that described in the parable of the wheat and the tares. The crucial additional element here, which is not present in the earlier parable, is the cessation of the work of general gathering, that is, the net must be drawn ashore before the selection of the good fish begins. And it is here that the distinction between the cleansing of the Sanctuary and the work of Harvest may be found. During the time of Harvest, and not before, the general proclamation of the Gospel ceases.

> The net was not intended to catch all the fish of the sea. Our Lord, the great Chief Fisherman, designed to catch a particular number of fish of a particular kind, no matter how many of the other varieties went into the net with them; and when the full number of the desired, peculiar kind, have entered the net it is ordered ashore for the purpose of sorting and separating. When the net is thus ordered ashore, the commission given at the beginning of the age, to cast the net into the sea (Matt. 28:19; 24:14), should be understood as at an end; and all who would continue to be co-workers with the Lord must give heed to his directions, and no longer give their time to general fishing, but the the present work of selecting and gathering.[19]

There is, then, no effective difference between the processes which constitute the cleansing of the Sanctuary on the one hand, and the separating work of the Harvest on the other. Nor is there any distinction to be drawn between the Sanctuary class as constituted in 1846 and the whole of the true Church. The crucial difference lies in the function of the Gospel proclamation, especially from 1881 which, as was noted above,[20] was the time when the general invitation to become joint heirs with Christ ceased. No longer is preaching for the purpose of making converts to Christianity; rather, its purpose is to seek to ensure that all who have already been called by God to be members of the true Church make good their response to that call and come out of Babylon, or nominal Christianity.

At the same time that the general 'high calling' of the Gospel age comes to an end, another general calling begins but this is to remain relatively insignificant during the Harvest. This is, the general call of the whole world to the Millennial blessings and favors upon conditions of faith and willing obedience. . . . This however, is a lower call, a less favor than that which ceased; – a call to enjoy blessings under the Kingdom, but not to be parts of the anointed, Kingdom class. And this *change* – this stopping of the higher favor and beginning of a lesser favor – will be little noticed in the present time. . . . As a matter of fact, then, the only ones who see clearly the pecularily high and grand features of the call of the Gospel age – the only ones , therefore, who could announce or explain this calling – are the very ones who are also shown from God's word that the time limit of this call was reached in Pctober, 1881. Others, while quoting the Apostle's words concerning a 'high calling of God in Christ,' really explain the lower call which belongs to the Millennial age. Hence the general Gospel call, the true one, is ended. None can extend it. [21]

Notes

1. C. T. Russell, *Thy Kingdom Come*, pp. 62f.

2. *Ibid.*, pp. 64ff.

3. Above, Chapter 3.

4. Russell, *op. cit.*, p. 83.

5. Louis F. Hartman and Alexander A. Di Lella, 'Daniel'in Raymond Brown *et al.* (eds), *The New Jerome Biblical Commentary* p. 419.

6. Russell, *op. cit.*, pp. 86ff.

7. *Ibid.*, p. 88.

8. *Ibid.*, pp. 92f.

9. Above, Chapter 4.

10. Above, Chapter 3.

11. Hartman and Di Lella, 'Daniel' in Raymond Brown *et al.* (eds), *The New Jerome Biblical Commentary,* p. 417.

12. Above, Chapter 5, note 10.

13. Russell, *op. cit.*, p. 107.

14. *Ibid.*, p. 108.

15. *Ibid.*, pp. 108f.

16. *Ibid.*, p. 119.
17. Above, Chapter 6.
18. Russell, *op. cit.*, p. 121; pp. 150ff.
19. *Ibid.*, p. 215.
20. Above, Chapter 6.
21. Russell, *op. cit.*, pp. 218f.

Chapter Nine
The End-time Calendar

Although there is some detail still to be added, the previous chapters complete the description of that complex basic framework of Russell's millennialist beliefs which I refer to as his end-time calendar. From time to time the exposition has proved to be, to some extent, repetitive. This reflects the fact, noted earlier,[1] that the system comprises, in effect, a complete system within a larger whole, and the fact that several of the major elements in the system have more than one derivation. It can now be seen, in fact, that the larger whole comprises two separate systems which have been fused together. A comparison of the two sub-systems will be useful before the completion of the whole picture with the final details.

Table 2 summarises the system expounded in *The Divine Plan of the Ages* and *The Time is at Hand*. Although it must be acknowledged that this is a kind of historicist system, it is important to recognise that is not historicism of the traditional kind. It borrows from that tradition some elements which had not previously occupied a central position in any system, but it borrows also from the dispensationalism of J. N. Darby. It is here, especially, that Russell's system is creative, for the borrowings, though recognisable as such, have received the distinctive treatment of Russell's movement.

To the foregoing sub-system there can be added another which, unlike the former, is not complete in itself. This system, summarised in Table 3, is clearly recognisable as a development within the historicist tradition and, as such, offers less scope than the former for innovation. Indeed, Russell's traditional historicism may be fairly described as a revision of Miller's system, its immediate predecessor in the tradition.

Unlike the systems from which it has sprung, however, this one is not complete, for it does not reach the great climax because Russell, unlike his predecessors, has separated this climax from the beginning of the Second Presence of Christ. As a revision of the tradition, this is the more vulnerable part of Russell's system. When future events fail to confirm this latest version, there being no further revisions readily available, this whole sub-system will have to be discarded.

Table 4 puts the two sub-systems together and summarises the whole of Russell's system. It is useful, however, to continue to regard the whole as two integrated systems, for it is in this that the durability of Russell's approach

Table 2.   *The Historicist Dispensational System*

Date	Description
1874 –	Second Presence of Christ begins
	Millennium begins
	Harvest begins
1878 –	Christ takes power as king
	Jews restored to favour
	Christendom rejected
1881 –	End of the 'high calling'
1914 –	End of the 'times of the Gentiles'

Table 3.   *The Traditional Historicist System*

Date	Description
1799	The 'time of the end' begins
	End of the 1,260 days
1829	End of the 1,290 days
	Unsealing of Daniel
1846	End of 2,300 days
	Sanctuary cleansed
1874	Second Presence of Christ begins
	Millennium begins
	End of the 1,335 days
	Harvest begins

Table 4.   *The Composite End-time Calendar*

Date	Description
1799	The 'time of the end' begins
	End of the 1,260 days
1829	End of the 1,290 days
	Unsealing of Daniel
1846	End of 2,300 days
	Sanctuary cleansed
1874	Second Presence of Christ begins
	Millennium begins
	End of the 1,335 days
	Harvest begins
1878	Christ takes power as king
	Jews restored to favour
	Christendom rejected
1881	End of the 'high calling'

lies. For, at the point where traditional historicist millennialism has reached the limit of its capacity for plausible revision, Russell has expounded a system from which that tradition can be discarded without leaving a void. If that complete system which remains following the discarding of traditional historicism should prove to be capable of plausible revision, then what will emerge after such revision is likely to prove a major step in the process of isolation. It will continue the process of isolation which has already been noted, and it will also distance itself from the very tradition within which it developed. The problem which this creates, however, lies in the fact that, historically, the Watch Tower movement itself straddles the very gulf which has thus been opened up.

Early Revision

The system described above will, obviously, require amendment in due course, but it must be appreciated that already, during the early years of the Watch Tower movement, there had to be significant trial and error. In particular, the question when the last remaining members of the Church, the body of Christ, would receive their change from human form to heavenly glory, proved to be troublesome (as, indeed, it was to be in later years). It had been the view of the original group to which Russell belonged that 1878 would be the year when the saints would be carried away to heaven. The failure of that expectation led to division within the group. Russell developed the explanation, which was retained in his fully developed system, that 1878 was the year when all the saints who had previously died were resurrected and that thereafter all would be transformed to heavenly glory immediately upon their death.[2] Indeed, in *Thy Kingdom Come*, Russell in one place points out that all the saints will have to pass through death to receive their heavenly reward.[3] Nelson Barbour, however, could not agree with this explanation of the failure of 1878 and this, together with disagreement over the interpretation of the doctrine of the atonement, led him to separate from Russell.

Russell's belief, as expressed in *Thy Kingdom Come*, was that the last of the saints would not be taken to heaven until immediately before the climax of 1914,[4] but before arriving at this view he had expected 1881 to see the glorification of the saints.[5] This continuing conviction that there would come a time when all who remained would be changed to heavenly glory does seem to contradict the view that all must pass through death. Finally, the separation of the ideas of the end of the 'high calling' and the glorification of the saints allowed the retention of 1881 in the system together with a more distant reward.

The importance of these revisions lies not in their significance for the system as a whole, for the changes which they make are not fundamental. Rather, their importance lies in the fact that this comparatively brief period of trial and error led to the schism between Russell and his original associates. Within a year of the second failed expectation, only Russell remained of the original leaders to continue promoting the system which had been developed within the group.[6] It was at this point, then, that he emerged as sole leader of the Watch Tower movement. At the same time, he was the movement's last effective link with the tradition from which the doctrines had derived; any further revisions after Russell's death would have to be undertaken by leaders with a much more restricted breadth of vision.

A Second Appraisal

Before proceeding to a detailed picture of the events that Russell actually believed would constitute the final climax of the present age and the inauguration of the earthly phase of the Kingdom of God, it is appropriate to make a second appraisal of his work. It is particularly useful to do so at this point in order to make clear what is not usually evident to the modern observer. Russell's system occupies a transitional place in the history of millennialism; it is firmly rooted in the Protestant mainstream, but its development established its position well within the sectarian fringe. The completed framework, as outlined so far, is inseparably linked with its antecedents, whereas the final details of the picture strain the relationship to the point of breaking.

Although Russell's system is a direct descendant of the Adventism of William Miller, it is important to recognise that it is also contemporary with the Adventism of Joseph Bates and Ellen White and, indeed, with the Christadelphian system of John Thomas as expounded in *Elpis Israel*. Thomas's system, though obviously in the same tradition as Russell and Adventism, appears to have exerted no influence upon Russell and, in fact, differs from both Russell and Adventism in ways which render it distinctive. Though Thomas's system took its place within the tradition during the same period as the emergence of Seventh-day Adventism and the Watch Tower movement, it cannot, unlike those, be regarded as a reaction to the failure of Miller's system or as arising from the disarray which followed the disappointment of 1844. Thomas described himself as having been all along an opponent of Millerism.[7] The significant differences from Miller's and Russell's place within the tradition lie in the fact that he considered the period leading to the cleansing of the sanctuary, following a Septuagint rendering, to be 2,400 years beginning with the decree of Cyrus for the rebuilding of the Temple in 540 BC, not the decree of Artaxerxes in in 457 or 454 BC; the sanctuary to be cleansed was not the Church but the land of Israel; Thomas identified two periods of 1,260 years: the first, beginning with the establishment of the Church state in AD 313 ends with the St Bartholomew massacre in AD 1572; the second is the more familiar application to the period from the establishment of the papacy to the Napoleonic era.

The late nineteenth-century snapshot of millennialism, then, presents a very different picture from that of the disarray during the years immediately following the failure of Miller's system. The Christadelphianism of John Thomas, which had its beginnings during Miller's time, has become established; and out of the disarray following the disappointment of 1844, Seventh-day Adventism and the Watch Tower movement have emerged. These three movements now represent virtually the whole of the continuing historicist tradition which has become almost entirely confined to the sectarian fringe of the Church. This isolation has been the result of three factors: the developing ecclesiologies of the three movements have tended to identify their millennialist systems as their own peculiar property, separate from the mainstream; secondly, once the main examples of the tradition are seen to be the preserve of the fringe, it is only a short step before system-building itself of this sort is also seen to belong to the fringe; and thirdly, the possibility of constructing alternative systems is by this time severely limited.

From its earliest beginnings, the historicist tradition proceeded by trial and error but, before the nineteenth century, it was largely a matter of the interpretation of small parts of the whole. With the nineteenth century there begins the blossoming of whole systems of interpretation which build upon the ideas developed earlier. At this point the trial and error takes on two different aspects: there is minor amendment to systems which have failed the test of time, such as for example, the Seventh-day Adventist revision of Miller's system or the present-day Christadelphian amendment of Thomas's system; and there is the large-scale replacement of one system for another, such as for example, Russell's replacement of Miller's system or, as will be seen later, the twentieth-century Watch Tower replacement of Russell's system.

From the vantage point of the late twentieth century the judgement that Russell's system has failed appears obvious. To his nineteenth-century opponents in the Christian mainstream it may have seemed inevitable that it would fail. But among his many adherents, the credibility of the system did not require gullibility or lack of intelligence. Indeed, a significant part of the appeal of the system is to intelligence. The three volumes of *Studies in the Scriptures* which have been considered so far comprise about a thousand pages of fairly closely argued text. To be persuaded, then, requires some considerable effort of assimilation, assessment and understanding. The whole system is internally coherent; it does not violate its own rules of interpretation nor does it contain any significant self-contradictions. It appeared to have external confirmation of both its major rule of interpretation and some of its historical applications. That is, both the year-for-a-day principle and its application, especially in the case of the seventy weeks and the 1,260 days, were apparently justified by historical events. And it is worth noting that the credibility of the system need not be undermined by putting it within its place in the tradition, that is, as the latest attempt where all others had failed, for it can, with some justification, be seen as explaining the reason for the failure of its immediate predecessor in the tradition.

At this point it is interesting to note that Russell's contemporary opponents seem to have focused their attention not on his millennialist beliefs, but upon his other heterodox views and his alleged personal failings. Modern polemicists usually follow the same path. Consequently, Martin and Klann, for example, can say:

'Jehovah's Witnesses' is simply a pseudonym for 'Russellism' or 'Millennial Dawnism.' The similarity of the two systems is more than coincidental or accidental, regardless of the Witnesses' loud shouts to the contrary.[8]

In fact, so far as the doctrine of the Millennium is concerned, the dissimilarity between Russell and the Witnesses is at least as great as that between Russell and Miller. But the doctrine of the Millennium has rarely received more than cursory attention, and the result is that commentators tend to give the impression of far greater eccentricity than is the case. So Hoekema, for example, having briefly described the application of the year-for-a-day principle to Nebuchadnezzar's vision of the tree, sums it up thus:

By a calculation which involves a conglomeration of figures derived with great ingenuity from assorted passages taken from Luke, Daniel, Revelation, and Ezekiel, we have arrived at the year 1914. Here is 'knight jump exegesis' with a vengeance![9]

Apparently, Hoekema is unaware of the long pedigree of the method which he ridicules. Gruss, on the other hand, acknowledges the antiquity of the method but regards its Christian origins within the Roman Catholic Church as good reason to be suspicious. Nor does he seem to be aware of those apparent successes which might have suggested some qualification to his statement that all who have attempted to apply the method have failed in their predictions.[10]

Given the fact that, in constructing his system, Russell employed a method which had previously exercised the talents of theologians whose orthodoxy and good sense were never in question, it is pertinent to ask what, apart from its eventual failure, apart from his other beliefs, and apart from his personal affairs, might have so undermined the credibility of his system as to render it unworthy of serious consideration even before the failure of its predictions. I would argue that when the question is put in this way, Russell has to be ranked alongside all his predecessors in the tradition. His system does not represent any significant migration towards eccentricity. But if that is the case, then it is perhaps necessary to reconsider the question why historicist premillennialism moved out to the sectarian fringe. The answer which has been assumed so far, namely that increasing ridicule following successive failures prompted a closing of ranks and, consequently, a tendency to develop their own ecclesiologies among continuing historicists, represents, perhaps, only one aspect of the question. If the most vitriolic criticism of these movements concentrated then, as now, not upon their millennialism but upon their other beliefs, then that is where a major cause of isolation must lie. This raises the question whether heterodoxy had become a necessary factor in the survival of historicism. That is, could a historicist premillennial system alone have proved a sufficient basis for the formation of a movement outside the mainstream? Conversely, if the millennialist component were to disappear from such a movement, could the heterodoxy which originally provided the vehicle for that millennialism be sufficient to sustain the movement? It is questions such as these that must be addressed when considering in what form the Watch Tower movement might survive in the long term.

Notes

1. Above, Chapter 6.
2. M. J. Penton, *Apocalypse Delayed*, p. 23.
3. C. T. Russell, *Thy Kingdom Come*, p. 238.
4. *Ibid.*, p. 228.
5. Penton, *op. cit.*, p. 24.
6. *Ibid.*, p. 24.
7. John Thomas, *Chronikon Hebraikon*, p. 35, in John Thomas, *Elpis Israel*.
8. W. Martin and N. Klann, *Jehovah of the Watchtower*, p. 41.
9. A. Hoekema, *Jehovah's Witnesses*, p. 43.
10. Edmond C. Gruss, *The Jehovah's Witnesses and Prophetic Speculation*, pp. 44ff.

Chapter Ten
The Battle of Armageddon

The previous chapter concluded with a running assessment of Russell's millennialist system. The reason for interpolating an assessment at that stage of the enquiry is that it might the more clearly show Russell's ideas in the context of the tradition within which they had grown rather than within the context of subsequent events. Turning to *The Battle of Armageddon*, the fourth volume of *Studies in the Scriptures*, a further reason why this was appropriate becomes apparent. The previous volumes in the series were generally well written and easy to read. Volume 4 is somewhat different. Large sections of it amount to a compendium of frequently very lengthy quotations, sometimes whole articles, from contemporary sources illustrative of Russell's view of the world on the threshold of Armageddon. Those chapters which are not dependent upon other sources for the bulk of their material display a style of writing which is never as easily readable as the previous volumes, and is often quite tedious.

One reason for the distinct change of style with the fourth volume of the series may lie in the fact that hitherto Russell had the cooperation of his wife, Maria, in the writing of his books and articles. From about 1894 the relationship between them began to break down, resulting, in November 1897, in separation. During this period Maria Russell's attitude towards her husband changed from loyalty to outright hostility. The publication of *The Battle of Armageddon* in 1897, then, roughly coincided with the final rift between Russell and his co-author. That the Russells had been engaged in increasingly acrimonious quarrelling during the time when *The Battle of Armageddon* was in preparation would lead one to surmise that their working relationship must have been undermined. So the distinct change of style of the fourth volume of the series strongly suggests that it is, for the first time, Russell's own largely unaided work. But Maria Russell's departure at this point should not be seen as implying that hitherto the literature may have expressed her views rather than those of her husband. Indeed, one of the causes of her discontent was the fact that Russell did not allow the publication of any opinions other than his own. Nevertheless, her influence upon Russell's work probably extended beyond its literary style, though how far it is perhaps not possible to determine.[1]

A second reason for the poorer literary quality of *The Battle of Armageddon* may be found in the fact that in the preceding three volumes of the series Russell had already written all that was necessary for a full exposition of his beliefs about the Second Presence of Christ, the Millennium and the Kingdom of God. To provide a further volume which adds nothing of substance to the doctrine and does not explore new areas, called for the exercise of talents which Russell did not possess. From a purely literary point of view, better use of the material of the fourth volume could have been made by drastic pruning and the incorporation of what remained into perhaps only slightly enlarged editions of the preceding volumes.

The Battle of Armageddon, however, does provide an important insight into the nineteenth-century Watch Tower movement. The credibility of the historicist tradition in general was being steadily undermined by the widening gulf between the apparent fulfilment of some parts of the prophetic material at the end of the eighteenth century, and the onset of its final phase. *The Battle of Armageddon*, however, bridged that gulf by providing a detailed description of late nineteenth-century political, economic and ecclesiastical affairs, and their anticipated outcome, in terms of the doctrinal system already expounded.

The Gathering Storm

> I saw three unclean spirits like frogs come out of the mouth of the dragon, and out of the mouth of the beast, and out of the mouth of the false prophet. For they are the spirits of devils, working miracles, which go forth unto the kings of the earth and of the whole world, to gather them to the battle of that great Day of God Almighty. (Revelation 16:13,14)

Russell's interpretation of Revelation's symbolism draws upon the tradition which he has inherited and amends it in his own individual way. So the Dragon of Revelation 16 is understood to mean the Roman power and, hence, civil power in general wherever it is found, and the Beast represents the papacy. It is the Image of the Beast, which is elsewhere referred to as the False Prophet, that receives Russell's individual treatment; it represents the Evangelical Alliance.

> The Evangelical Alliance, an organization of the different Protestant denominations, was formed in 1846 for the very purpose of doing in their own way the same thing that Catholicism would do in its own way. Seeing the great power that Roman Catholics would exercise because of a united system, Protestants said, 'We are divided. We have no power. We will organize.' Then and there, according to the Scriptures, they made an Image of the Beast.[2]

Before the Image is able to operate, however, it must receive life, or authorisation, from the two-horned beast (Revelation 13:15). That is, the Protestant denominations, being outside the original apostolic succession, have no effective authority to preach. This situation Russell expected to be remedied when, in due course, the Church of England, which was symbolised by the two-horned beast, would give the Evangelical Alliance apostolic authority to preach. Thereafter the Alliance would be in a powerful position.

The Scriptures clearly indicate that the Image of the Beast is to get so great power that it will do the same thing that the Roman Catholic Church did in the past; and that the two systems, Catholic and Protestant, will rule the civilized world with a high hand through the civil power – the Dragon.[3]

The processes which culminate in the time of great trouble marking the onset of the Battle of Armageddon amount to something like the class struggle of revolutionary politics – but with a very different outcome. The unclean spirits like frogs symbolise the doctrines or policies of the three bodies from which they emanate. Essentially they are conservative and have the purpose of preserving the *status quo* and preventing revolution.

Out of the mouth of the Dragon comes the doctrine of the Divine right of Kings: 'Do not look back of the curtain of history to see where kings got that right. Accept the doctrine; for if you do not, and if men look into the matter, there will be a terrible revolution and everything will go down!' The Beast and the False Prophet have similar croakings. The Catholic Church says, 'Do not look behind! Do not question anything about the Church!' Protestantism says, also, 'We are great, we are wise, we know a great deal. Keep quiet! No one will then know that you know nothing.' All say (croaking), 'We tell you that if you say anything against present arrangements, terrible things will come to pass.'[4]

The anti-revolutionary policies of Church and state will lead eventually to the suppression of all the new freedoms which the masses of ordinary people had come to enjoy and to take for granted by the late nineteenth century, but the result of that desperate measure will be anarchy on a global scale.

So, with world history having less than two decades before the final consummation, all the actors in the final drama are clearly identified: The majority of the members of the 'little flock' are with the Lord in heaven whilst the remnant of that body, the cleansed Sanctuary, are engaged in the work of the Harvest. Babylon the Great is now seen to comprise the whole of Christendom, not just the Roman Catholic Church, and together with the civil governments of the world, symbolised by the Dragon, is strongly resisting the processes which will lead, inexorably, to the establishment of the earthly phase of the Kingdom of God. The masses of the people, though they do not know it, will be used by God as his great army (Joel 2:1-11) to overthrow the power of the Beast, the False Prophet and the Dragon.

Establishing the Kingdom

It has already been seen that an important feature of the preparation for the earthly phase of the kingdom is the restoration of the Jews to Palestine.[5] As events reached their climax, this would become the main focus of attention. At the time of writing *The Battle of Armageddon*, Russell observed a steady flow of Jewish immigrants to Palestine in confirmation of his beliefs. But that steady flow needed to increase:

All men are witnesses to the fact that such a gathering of Israel to Palestine is begun, but it is quite manifest that their exodus from other lands will have to receive some great and sudden impulse in order to accomplish this prophecy within the appointed time. Just what that impulse will be remains yet to be seen.[6]

By the time the final storm is about to break, the people of Israel will be settled in Palestine in vast numbers and will be enjoying considerable prosperity and peace. They will not at first, however, understand their place in the divine plan. When the time of trouble does begin it will involve, first, the nations of Christendom and then all nations of the world. And the final, decisive phase will involve Israel. This will be in fulfilment of the prophecy of Ezekiel 38:11-23 which tells of the hosts of Gog and Magog coming against the prosperous but apparently defenceless Israelites who are resettled in their homeland. The invading armies are defeated when God intervenes on behalf of his people.

So the Battle of Armageddon begins in Christendom when the masses of the people revolt against the oppression of Church and state; similar revolution rapidly spreads throughout the rest of the world. Then, prompted by jealousy and the prospect of easy plunder, the anarchic forces turn their attention to the peaceful and wealthy Israelites. Finally, as the prophecy has indicated, God will step in to bring the time of trouble to an end.

> In the midst of the trouble God will reveal himself as Israel's defender as in ancient times, when his favor was with them nationally. Their extremity will be his opportunity; – and there their blindness will be removed.[7]

The miraculous deliverance of Israel is but the beginning of the process whereby first Israel and at last the whole world are brought to the realisation of what is happening. About the time of Israel's deliverance, or immediately thereafter, the 'ancient worthies' – the patriarchs and prophets of the pre-Christian period – will be resurrected and will make themselves known to the regathered Israelites. Being resurrected to perfection, the genuineness of their claims will be immediately apparent.

> When God's time for the inauguration of his Kingdom among men shall arrive, his agents will all be amply ready for the service; and their master strokes of wise policy, their moderation and dignified self-control, and their personal exemplification of every grace and virtue will attract men and quickly enlist them – chastened under the great tribulation – in active cooperation. Even before the disclosure of their identity, doubtless the people of Israel will have remarked their preeminence over other men.[8]

The 'ancient worthies' will then form a righteous government which the people will recognise at once as being of the Lord. They will then learn, further, that the real kingdom over them is the spiritual, heavenly kingdom with the crucified Jesus as king and at that point the removal of their blindness will be complete.

Meanwhile, the rest of the world, still in disarray following the time of trouble and observing all that is happening in Palestine, will begin to realise that the new government there has the answer to the rest of the world's problems.

> Whether impostors or not, the work of these men who claim to be the resurrected prophets is the very one the world needs! Would to God they would take control of the whole world, and bring order and peace out of our universal disorder. And then they will send to have these

wonderful 'princes' extend everywhere their government, their yoke of righteousness, seen to be so beneficial to Israel. This is stated by the Prophet in the following words: 'It shall come to pass in the last days, that the mountain [Kingdom] of the Lord's house shall be established in the top of the mountains [as a Kingdom overtopping or overruling all kingdoms], and shall be exalted above the hills [the highest peaks]; and all nations shall flow unto it. And many people shall go and say, Come ye, and let us go up to the mountain [Kingdom] of the Lord, to the house of the God of Jacob; and *he will teach us of his ways*, and we will walk in his paths. For out of Zion [the spiritual Kingdom – the glorified Christ, head and body] shall go forth the law, and the word of the Lord from Jerusalem [the seat of the earthly representative government in the hands of the 'princes']. And [previously – in the great time of trouble] he shall judge among the nations, and shall rebuke many people. And [as a result of the Lord's rebukes and subsequently his law and Word] they shall beat their swords into plowshares, and their spears into pruning hooks: nation shall not lift up sword against nation, neither shall they learn war any more.' – Isa 2:2-4; Micah 4:1-4.[9] (Parentheses and italics original)

The earthly phase of the kingdom of God, then, begins at once to restore order to a strife-torn world. Not only are the imperfect and wicked institutions of the world removed and replaced by righteous systems, but the people themselves also begin to experience physical restoration as all forms of ill health gradually become a thing of the past. This, together with the resurrection of the 'ancient worthies', will suggest at last to the people the possibility of resurrection of the dead generally. So the resurrection will begin in response to the prayers of the people and eventually all who have died,

> even the hosts of Gog and the sinners in Israel which will have perished in the battle of the great day, shall in due time come forth.[10]

As the work of the millennial kingdom proceeds, the earth is brought to the state of perfection which God had originally intended. At the close of the Millennium Satan, who has been restrained since his defeat at Armageddon, is to be released for a short while during what Russell describes as a 'harvest' of the millennial age. But where the Harvest of the Gospel age had gathered in only a 'little flock', the results will be reversed at the close of the Millennium. All mankind having been brought to perfection and having seen the miraculous transformation of the world into a paradise, very few will thereafter submit to the temptation to follow Satan. Satan, all his demons and those few who succumb will finally suffer everlasting destruction. Then Christ will hand back the kingdom to Jehovah and Edenic perfection will be guaranteed for all eternity.[11]

Conclusions

With the foregoing summary of *The Battle of Armageddon*, this survey of Russell's millennialist beliefs comes to an end. Although the fourth volume of the series added nothing of any substance to the system which had not already received some mention in earlier volumes, the details which Russell now supplies foreshadow some of the significant developments which were to take place during the following years in the beliefs and affairs of the Watch Tower movement. The fact that so much detail has been given of the expected historical developments during the closing years of the 'times of the Gentiles' and the events constituting the climax, makes it the more difficult to reinterpret the system when those events do not occur. So long as a system is expounded in which the key events are referred to in the vocabulary supplied by the tradition with only minimal elaboration, then there may remain scope for reapplying the whole system, with its vocabulary redefined as necessary, before the pressure to begin reassigning dates becomes irresistible. So, for example, following the failure of Miller's system, because it seemed to some that there remained a question concerning the exact definition of the 'cleansing of the sanctuary', it was possible to offer a new definition of the sanctuary. That being accepted, it became possible to retain the whole of Miller's system but with some terms rather differently defined.

In Russell's case, however, it does seem that by providing a wealth of detail he has made amendments of this kind improbable. Three key ideas in particular have been so thoroughly defined as to make it impossible to allow the eventual outcome of history to determine more precisely the meanings of those ideas. So the restoration of Israel cannot without difficulty be understood as anything other than the return of the Jewish people to Palestine; the 'times of the Gentiles', similarly, have been firmly bonded to the idea of the restoration of Israel; and the time of great trouble has been defined as a conflict between the masses of the people and the institutions of Church and state.

The greater complexity and detail of Russell's system, then, will require that either the system be retained largely unamended or, if revision is found to be irresistible, it will need thoroughgoing amendments both in the definitions and in the end-time calendar. However, if retention is made possible by relegating the prophetic doctrine to a position where it attracts only the attention of those adherents with a special interest, then the whole character of the movement will be changed and it will become, as it never was for Russell, a movement occupying the gap noted above[12] between the start of the end-time fulfilment and its resumption and completion. Almost inevitably, then, the Watch Tower movement is one which must keep on updating itself in order to keep bridging the gulf which is always threatening to become impossibly wide.

Not only does the elaboration of Russell's system impose severe constraints upon the way in which it may later be amended, it also points forward to a new and important factor in the process of isolation of the Watch Tower movement. In developing his ideas concerning the processes which culminate in the battle of Armageddon, Russell appears to borrow from contemporary political thinking the idea of revolution by the downtrodden masses. So the 'Lord's great army' at the battle of Armageddon is defined in distinctly revolutionary terms. It is not the saints, but a very different class altogether.

In these very measures for self-defence devised by 'the powers that be,' there is probably a snare which they do not realize. The armies upon which they depend, be it remembered, are the armies of the common people: these millions of disciplined warriors have wives and sons and daughters and brothers and sisters and cousins and friends in the ranks of the common people, with whose interests their own are linked by nature's strong ties; and their service of thrones and kingdoms is only secured by imperative orders. . . . Year by year these armed hosts are less and less infatuated with the 'glory' of war, more keenly alive to its sufferings and privations, and less and less devoted to the sovereign powers that command their services. . . . All of these are indications of at least a possibility that in the crisis approaching the mighty armed and disciplined hosts of Christendom may turn their power against the authorities that called them into being. . . . Just what conditions and circumstances will be used of the Lord as his 'voice' of command to marshal this mighty army we may not now be able to clearly surmise; but we live in a day which makes history rapidly; and on general principles it would not be unreasonable to expect movements in this direction at any time.[13]

With views such as this it is not surprising that the movement was to experience intense popular and political opposition during the First World War, especially in Canada and the United States of America. That opposition virtually completed the movement's isolation which had begun during the early years of Russell's leadership. But as will become evident, it also provided some of the raw material for the reinterpretation of beliefs following the disillusionment of the war and its aftermath. It provided twentieth-century data for explanation in terms of a twentieth-century version of the doctrine.

Notes

1. M. J. Penton, *Apocalypse Delayed*, pp. 35ff.
2. C. T. Russell, *The Battle of Armageddon*, p. ix.
3. *Ibid.*, p. x.
4. *Ibid.*, p. xii.
5. Above, Chapter 5.
6. Russell, *op. cit.*, p. 553.
7. *Ibid.*, p. 555.
8. *Ibid.*, pp. 626f.
9. *Ibid.*, pp. 628f.
10. *Ibid.*, p. 640.
11. *Ibid.*, pp. 644ff.
12. Above, Chapter 10.
13. Russell, *op. cit.*, pp. 545f.

Chapter Eleven
The End of an Era

As 1914 approached Russell became more cautious in his statements on prophecy. Nevertheless, although disclaiming inspiration and infallibility for his ideas, he remained confident in his system as a whole. If there should turn out to be any error in his end-time calendar, he believed, it would be fairly minor. So, for example, he conceded that the 'times of the Gentiles' might expire in 1914 or 1915 and he began to refer less to the clearly observable events which he had predicted than to the theoretical or spiritual ideas underlying them, such as the end of the Harvest period or the expiry of the lease of sovereignty to Gentile governments.[1]

Whereas future generations of Watch Tower adherents came to regard Russell's predictions as greatly successful, he and his contemporaries faced considerable difficulty when trying to interpret current affairs in the light of what they had expected. The completion of the Jewish resettlement of Palestine remained a long way off; the 'little flock' did not receive their heavenly reward; the denominations of the Evangelical Alliance remained outside the Apostolic Succession and were far from dominant in affairs of state throughout the world; and, although the First World War could well have been described as a time of great trouble, it was clearly not the 'time of great trouble' of prophecy as Russell had interpreted it, nor did it reach the culmination which he had expected. The outbreak of war in 1914, however, did provide a major world event that was capable of explanation in terms of a somewhat modified Watch Tower millennialism.

Russell died on 31 October 1916 and it was left to his successors to carry on the process, which he had begun, of adapting the system in order to encompass the unexpected delay of Armageddon beyond 1914. It had been Russell's hope that, following his own presidency, the leadership of the movement would become a collective responsibility. However, little more than two months after his death, the Society's shareholders elected Joseph Franklin Rutherford sole President.

Rutherford was born in 1869 in Missouri to Baptist parents. He trained as a lawyer under the apprentice system which was prevalent at that time in the United States of America. He joined the Watch Tower movement in 1906 and quickly established his usefulness to the organisation as a legal adviser and administrator. Unlike Russell, however, who had been generally friendly and gentle in his dealings with people, Rutherford was an abrasive man who frequently alienated those who did not agree with him. Out of deference to Russell, he chose not to assume the title 'Pastor' by which his predecessor had been known, even though some of the congregations of Bible Students did appoint him Pastor in succession to Russell.[2] Rather, he styled himself 'Judge' as he was technically entitled, having served from time to time in that capacity during his legal career.

Among the Society's directors there was considerable opposition to Rutherford's elevation to the presidency, so they sought to amend the Society's constitution in order to restrict the power of that office in keeping with Russell's wishes for the movement's continuing leadership. But because the dissenting directors, so Rutherford maintained, had been appointed by Russell without subsequently being confirmed in office, as they should have been, by the annual shareholders' meeting, he was able simply to remove them and substitute his own appointees.[3]

The Finished Mystery

One of Rutherford's first actions as President, whilst he was engaged in the power struggle to establish his position, was, without reference either to his fellow directors or to the editorial committee which Russell had nominated in his will, to commission a seventh volume of *Studies in the Scriptures*. Responsibility for preparing this volume was given to two of Russell's close associates, George H. Fisher and Clayton J. Woodworth. On the face of it, their brief was to edit for publication the notes left by Russell, who had intended to publish a seventh volume at some stage, and to draw upon his published writings in order to provide a commentary on the books of Revelation, the Song of Solomon and Ezekiel. Working entirely separately, Fisher prepared the section on Ezekiel and Woodworth prepared the sections on Revelation and the Song of Solomon. The completed volume was published in July 1917 under the title *The Finished Mystery*, and was described as the posthumous work of Russell, even though it was evidently widely realised amongst the Bible Students, as the movement's adherents had become known, that he had not been working on the seventh volume. In 1914 he had replied to a question about that volume:

> You will have to ask me something easier. I do not know, my dear friends, and I am not nearly as good a guesser as some of the rest of you . . . I am waiting for the Seventh Volume also. Waiting until it gets off the press – but I will tell privately, it is not on the press yet.[4]

And as late as 1916 his answer to a question about when he would write the seventh volume was:

> There are certain things we ought not to tell anyone; and amongst these are those things which we do not know.[5]

Publication of *The Finished Mystery* was not greeted with universal acclaim amongst the Bible Students. Dissent at this stage, however, appears to have centred upon the way in which Rutherford, it was claimed, exceeded his authority, rather than upon the amendments which were being put forward –

some of which, at least, had been initiated by Russell. Posthumous ascription to Russell was not sufficient to mollify those who believed that no successor could fill the role of the movement's first President. Indeed, it is obvious, even upon a fairly cursory reading of *The Finished Mystery*, that it was not in any straightforward sense the result of editing Russell's papers; rather, it was in large measure the original work of Woodworth and Fisher at the behest of the new President. So the exaggerated assertions of Russell's greatness and uniqueness, which appear throughout the book, did little to reassure the more conservative elements in the movement. Rather, they may have seemed to describe the presidential style which Rutherford would make his own.

The Finished Mystery also provoked opposition from outside the movement. Its prominent use in the United States of America, Canada and Great Britain during the summer of 1917 in a campaign directed against the clergy for their support of the First World War, led to its being banned in Canada and in the United States of America and to the arrest and trial of eight of the Society's directors in the United States on charges of sedition under the American Espionage Act. In June 1918 those eight directors, including Rutherford, Woodworth and Fisher, were found guilty and sentenced to lengthy terms of imprisonment.

Whilst in prison, the eight directors were re-elected to office by the Watch Tower Society's annual meeting held in Pittsburgh in January 1919. By this time much of the opposition to Rutherford had evaporated. Those who had been most forthright in their dissent had seceded from the parent body and had formed the first of several independent groups of Bible Students which were established during this period. The waverers, on the other hand, had been brought round to Rutherford's support, for a time at least, by the portrayal of him and his fellow-directors as martyrs for the cause. At this stage, however, it could only appear a pyrrhic victory, for the movement did seem to be on the point of extinction. But in March 1919 the eight were released on bail by order of the Supreme Court of the United States and the following month the judgement against them was reversed. Finally, a year after their release, the charges against them were dropped by the United States government.[6] Then began the long process of rebuilding the Watch Tower movement.

It would be unfair to place the whole blame for the Society's troubles during the war upon the new leadership. Russell's *The Battle of Armageddon*, for all its literary failings, was a far more coherent statement of views which could have attracted charges of sedition than was the rambling and incoherent *The Finished Mystery*. Had Russell's volume been used to spearhead the Society's anti-war campaign, the response of state and populace was unlikely to have been any less hostile.

New Beginnings

If the new ideas put forward in *The Finished Mystery* should seem to represent a major step in the direction of eccentricity, then, in fairness to the Society's new leaders, it should be pointed out that Russell had, perhaps, prepared the ground for what was to follow. In a lengthy appendix to *Thy Kingdom Come*, he had elaborated a theory that the Great Pyramid of Gizeh had been built under divine direction and that its dimensions, when interpreted on the basis that one inch represented one year, confirmed the chronology found in Scripture. The theory did not originate with Russell. He attributed it to one Robert Menzies, and received the endorsement of Professor C. Piazzi Smyth, one-time Astronomer Royal for Scotland, for his exposition of the theory.[7]

The pyramid theory, however, remained a secondary part of Russell's system. Though it may have been one of the factors predisposing the second generation of Watch Tower leaders to search for chronological derivations by methods not established in the tradition, it cannot be regarded as the only such factor. More important seems to have been the increasing isolation of the movement from the historicist tradition. Consequently, as will become apparent in due course, some of the new directions in chronology demonstrate a failure to appreciate the logic of Russell's method. And some are quite simply eccentric, for they relate neither to anything which had gone before nor to anything which was to follow.

However, it is interesting to observe that the process of amendment which proceeded under Rutherford's oversight reflects a similar feature to Russell's amendment of Miller's system. Russell had believed that Miller's major mistake lay in his assumption that all the events of the end were to occur virtually simultaneously; Russell's system, then, in contradistinction, identified a sequence of events rather than a single end point. Similarly, *The Finished Mystery* takes all that was expected for 1914 and places it in a sequence extending several years beyond then. Where Russell had been systematic in the construction of his theories, however, his successors appear to have proceeded on an *ad hoc* basis.

The first of the chronological amendments put forward by Woodworth in *The Finished Mystery* is evidently attributable to Russell and is, indeed, one of only two which do not obviously strain the relationship with the founding system. This revision relates to the argument from parallel dispensations and is based upon the observation that the end of the Jewish state in Judaea came some three years later than the destruction of Jerusalem in AD 70:

JEWISH & CHRISTIAN PARALLELS
Jewish Nominal Church	Christian Nominal Church
AD 29-33	AD 1874-1878

'They knew not the time of their visitation'

AD 33-36	AD 1878-881

'The Most Holy anointed, Divine favor prolonged for three and a half years to complete the seventy weeks of favor promised to Israel, their rejection being deferred.'

AD 36-73	AD 1881-1918

'Because of the overspreading of abominations, He shall make it desolate, even until the consummation, or *utter destruction* – until all that God has predetermined, shall be accomplished. – Daniel 9:24-27.'

The foregoing is Pastor Russell's last expression on the subject of chronology. . . . The chronology as it appears in the STUDIES IN THE

SCRIPTURES is accurate. The year 1914 brought the end of the Times of the Gentiles, but not the end of the Harvest work. Have the teachings of the parallels lost their value? Not at all. The point not previously noticed is that the Jewish polity was not to be destroyed in Jerusalem only, but throughout all Judea. ... When the Lord gave his wonderful prophecy in which the destinies of nominal Fleshly Israel, nominal Spiritual Israel, and the Israel of God, are set forth ... he showed that the end of Fleshly Israel foreshadowed the end of Spiritual Israel. Fleshly Israel had three ends; the destruction of Jerusalem in A.D. 70, the complete subjugation of Judea, in A.D. 73, and the actual depopulation of the whole of Palestine in A.D. 135. Which did he mean should be the end that would be a guide to his followers? Not the end in A.D. 70 foreshadowing 1915; for the Harvest of the Gospel Age is still in progress. Not the end in A.D. 135 foreshadowing 1980; for the Harvest is the end. He must have meant the end in Judea.[8]

This revision is, on the face of it, a relatively minor amendment to what had previously been established. As such, it requires only the substitution of one date by another which was later seen to be the more strongly indicated. There is nothing at this point to suggest that any of the supporting argument was felt to be in need of revision. However, a very important new factor had been brought in by the apparently minor variation. This becomes evident when it is considered how this new detail may be incorporated into the tables set out above in Chapter 9. Table 4 presents no problem; 1918 can simply be added at the foot as the next event in the end-time calendar. But when it is given its place in that sub-system to which it belongs, a further amendment becomes necessary. As it is derived in *The Finished Mystery*, 1918 clearly belongs to the historicist dispensational sub-system outlined in Table 2. It belongs there, however, by appropriating an argument supporting 1914, which continues to be supported by its two applications of the year-for-a-day principle, but not now by any argument from parallel dispensations. 1914, then, is no longer a component of the historicist dispensational sub-system, but nor does it belong to the traditional historicist sub-system. With just one small amendment, 1914, the date which was gradually to take on a new significance for the Watch Tower movement, has been stripped of any close relationship with either of the traditions which had been of major importance in the construction of Russell's theories.

The 'time of great trouble', then, is understood to begin in 1914 and to culminate, in 1918, in the global anarchy which is to result in the final destruction of Christendom. This seems to be a natural development of the ideas which Russell had expressed in *The Battle of Armageddon*, where he envisaged the immediate cause of this event as the turning of the war-weary masses of the people against the institutions of Church and state.

By identifying the trouble prophesied in Daniel 12:1 with troubles referred to elsewhere, *The Finished Mystery* finds confirmation of the time to expect another of the delayed events of the end. Speaking of Jerusalem, or nominal Israel which typified Christendom, Isaiah 66:7 says: 'Before she travailed, she brought forth; before her pain came she was delivered of a man child.' The Babylonian exile represented God's judgement upon a delinquent nation and typified the coming final judgement upon Christendom.

But if nominal Zion's travail is due to occur in the Spring of 1918, and if we are now but the 'one day' (one year) distant from that event which the Prophet mentions, what should be our expectation regarding the experience of the 'little flock' meantime? . . . The marvellous thing the Prophet here has to record is that a Man-child is to be born out of Zion before this travail comes. The birth of the body of Christ had its beginning with the inauguration of the first resurrection in 1878, before the trouble on Christendom began in 1914. Likewise the birth of the body will be completed before the end of the trouble on Christendom. This is a striking reference to the fact, elsewhere clearly taught, that the ripe wheat of the Gospel Church is to be separated from the tares, that they are to be exalted and glorified before the burning, the consuming trouble, shall come upon the latter.[9]

A second indication that 1918 would see the glorification of the remaining members of the 'little flock' was found in the fact that Christ's ascension occurred forty days after his resurrection. Applying the year-for-a-day principle, this period is shown to represent the forty years between the beginning of the resurrection of the sleeping saints in 1878 and the completion of that process in 1918.[10]

It is at this point that the first clear evidence of failure to understand the methods which Russell had used may be noted. In his system, all those events of Christ's first advent and immediately thereafter which had prophetic significance for the end time, yielded their time indications upon the basis of the argument from parallel dispensations. What is now put forward is the application of a method which belongs to the traditional historicist sub-system, to an element which belongs in the dispensational sub-system. The problem which this creates is not simply one for the commentator; it is a difficulty within the resulting system. In the dispensational sub-system, a whole sequence of events in the foreshadowing dispensation is related to a corresponding sequence in the fulfilling dispensation, in which the same intervals are observed. By treating a single event differently from all the rest, this correspondence has been damaged. Further, no reason is given why the interval between Christ's resurrection and his ascension, but not any other interval in the sequence, should be treated this way. The problem signals the start of a long process of trial and error which was to lead eventually to an entirely new set of beliefs concerning the inauguration of the Millennium.

Beyond 1918

With *The Finished Mystery* there began to emerge to a place of significance an idea which Russell had broached but which he had never pursued to any depth. Revelation 7, having referred to the 'little flock' as a company of 144,000 taken from the twelve tribes of Israel, then speaks of a 'great company' standing before the heavenly throne. Russell identified these as the ones who, having received the same call as members of the 'little flock', failed to make good that call because of lack of zeal.

They do come off victors in the end, as is shown by the fact that to them are granted the palm branches; but their lack of zeal hindered them from being accepted as of the overcoming class, thus preventing their eternal joint-heirship and glory as participants in the New Creation. . . . The place to which they will attain, as we have previously seen, will apparently be one similar in many respects to the estate or plane of the angels.[11]

In contrast to this, the 'great company' is now seen to have a significant part to play. Indeed, to them falls the responsibility of continuing the work of preaching for some time following the glorification of the last members of the 'little flock.'[12]

How long this supplementary preaching will continue is suggested by the observation that 'it seems to be the Heavenly Father's way to accomplish His work by weeks and half weeks'.[13] So the seven days when Noah was in the Ark awaiting the beginning of the flood (Genesis 7:4) represent the seven years from 1914 to 1921, the mid point of which sees the glorification of the 'little flock' and the end of which is marked by 'great company's' removal to heaven. In support of the idea that 1918 marks the mid-point of a seven-year 'week', there is listed a series of events which occurred midway between pairs of other events. For example, the covenant with Abraham was midway between the fall of Adam and the conversion of Cornelius; and Jesus' death in AD 33 was midway between his baptism in AD 29 and the conversion of Cornelius in AD 36.[14] The argument seems less than persuasive, however, since few of the relevant periods listed are multiples of seven or of three-and-a-half, so that it is not clear how they can be said to support the principle of weeks and half weeks.

Russell had envisaged the work of another class of people following the glorification of the 'little flock'. Having identified Elijah as a prophetic type of the Church during the close of the Gospel age, it was natural to see Elisha, Elijah's successor, as a type of those who would, in effect, be successors to the true Church. Russell, however, did not develop this idea and appears to have placed Elisha's antitype during the period immediately following the battle of Armageddon and not to have identified it with the 'great company.'[15] In *The Finished Mystery* there has been introduced an interval between the glorification of the 'little flock' and the establishment of the earthly phase of the kingdom of God. It is during this interval that the work of the Elisha class is now placed and the identity with the 'great company' is made.[16]

The time for the establishment of the earthly phase of the kingdom is given by a reworking of the calculation of the Jubilees. Russell had counted fifty times fifty years from the time when observance of the typical Jubilees ceased, and identified 1875 as the final year of that great cycle. But 1875 was, in effect, replaced by the antitype, the Millennium, which was therefore seen to begin in the autumn of 1874. He had an alternative way of arriving at that date and it is the alternative which was later to be modified. This is based upon the idea that God had ordained a total of seventy Jubilees following which the Millennium would be inaugurated:

> To fulfil the word of the Lord by the mouth of Jeremiah, until the land had enjoyed her sabbaths: for as long as she lay desolate she kept sabbath, to fulfil threescore and ten years. (2 Chronicles 36:21)

That is, the seventy years of exile in Babylon are an enforced observance of all the Jubilees which had been decreed. Now, it has already been seen that nineteen Jubilees had been observed, albeit imperfectly, prior to the exile.

The fifty-one which remained of the seventy, Russell calculated on the assumption that each cycle lacked its fiftieth year, the Jubilee. So counting fifty-one times forty-nine (2,499) years from 625 BC, the year of the nineteenth Jubilee, he arrived at AD 1874 as the end of the whole cycle.[17]

If the introduction at this stage of a cycle of seventy Jubilees should seem to make Russell's argument needlessly complicated and give rise to the suspicion that one fifty-year cycle has been omitted from the first calculation without sufficient explanation, then the reworking in *The Finished Mystery* will appear to simplify matters. For what is offered now is a straightforward calculation of seventy times fifty (3,500) years which begin in 1575 BC, as before, and end in 1925. The matter is dealt with expeditiously with none of Russell's complex arithmetic:

> There is evidence that the establishment of the Kingdom in Palestine
> will probably be in 1925, ten years later than we once calculated.
> The seventy Jubilees, reckoned as fifty years each, expire in October
> 1925.[18]

1925, then, takes its place in the revised system by appropriating an argument which had established 1874 in the original system. The modified argument, however, is offered as a reason for amending the significance of 1914, a date to which the original version had never applied, rather than 1874. The earlier date retains its place because it continues to be supported by the argument from parallel dispensations and the 1,335 days of Daniel 12:12, but its significance has been altered for, in so far as the Millennium is regarded as the antitypical Jubilee, it cannot now be held to have begun in 1874. But that fact is not yet explicitly acknowledged. Indeed, Woodworth continued to regard 1874 as the beginning of the Millennium[19] whereas Fisher, rather confusedly, both confirmed the earlier date,[20] and also placed the Millennium's beginning at some point still in the future.[21]

Having presented his revision of the Jubilee calculation, Woodworth then offers a further derivation of 1925. As the covenant with Abraham points forward to the blessings of the Millennium, he looks there for an indication of when the promise was to be fulfilled. This is to be found in the account of the sacrifices offered by Abraham in acknowledgement of the covenant:

> Genesis 15:1 - 16:3, read connectedly, indicates that Abraham's vision
> as to when he would receive the Kingdom was not granted until ten
> years after the covenant was made, or 2035 B.C. The ages of the
> animals offered aggregated eleven years, which, applied prophetically,
> on the scale of a year for a day, equal 3960 years, the length of time
> from the date of the visions to A.D. 1925.[22]

It is at this point especially that one of the difficulties of giving serious consideration to the arguments presented in *The Finished Mystery* becomes most acute. Hitherto, the method has proceeded by identifying periods, which may be either periods mentioned as such in prophecy, or an interval between a prophetically significant event at the close of the Jewish age and its counterpart at the close of the Gospel age. In the first case, the year-for-a-day principle applies; in the second case the argument from parallel dispensations may apply. In each instance, a period in Scripture indicates a corresponding period in the fulfilment. But what is now offered is simply a number which cannot be related to any period in the prophetic type from which it is taken. The result is an arbitrary calculation which purports to take its justification from an entirely different process. The interpretation of Genesis 15, then, does not relate to the methods which Russell had employed but belongs rather with the numerical speculations which both Woodworth and Fisher indulged in and which are found throughout their book.[23]

An Alternative Way Forward

Fisher's modification of the end-time calendar differed markedly from that of Woodworth and must be treated as a separate enterprise. Whereas Woodworth had amended some of the earlier calculations to construct his extension of the calendar, Fisher's contribution found new scriptures and new arguments to chart the course of events leading to the establishment of the kingdom.

The commentary on Ezekiel begins with the observation that the start of the prophet's visionary career in his thirtieth year corresponds with the beginning of Russell's understanding of the prophetic corpus at about the same age. Ezekiel, then, was a type of Russell[24] and references to his career are therefore found throughout the book, but it would be tedious to consider these in any detail. The commentary on some passages, however, deserves attention.

Ezekiel 4 had all along been a keynote passage for the historicist tradition, for it is there that the year-for-a-day principle is found. But apart from this it seems never to have furnished significant details in any scheme of interpretation. In *The Finished Mystery* Fisher offered an explanation of this chapter which comes close to the standard set by the most plausible examples of its kind in the tradition. The prophet was instructed by God to depict a siege against Jerusalem, lying first on his left side for three hundred and ninety days and then on his right side for forty days. During these periods the prophet, with an 'iron wall' between him and the city, is said to bear, first, the sin of the house of Israel and then the sin of the house of Judah.

In antitype, when both Israel and Judah are mentioned, and the prophecy is intended for an antitypical fulfilment, Israel signifies the Papacy and Judah signifies established Protestantism. . . . Priestcraft of the larger division of Christendom was to be under attack for 390 years, during which time the besieging elements, the reformers, were to be protected from Papacy by the 'iron wall' of the civil powers. This began in 1528 and ends in 1918. The year 1528 is one of the turning points of history. Protestantism in England and Germany was in the balance. The sudden rise of Charles V of Germany to great power had emboldened Pope Clement to side with Charles. He induced the Emperor to support a measure designed to limit the spread of Protestantism, to be followed by its utter destruction. . . . Philip Landgrave of Saxony discovered the plot, took arms, and in 1528 forced indemnity from a Catholic bishop. . . .

The house of Judah represents Protestantism, the Protestant churches. Until 1878, when cast off by the returned and present Messiah, Protestantism enjoyed Divine favor, just as the two tribes, collectively called Judah, did as compared with the idolatrous ten tribes of Israel. After 1874 the Present Truth took the form of a general overhauling of creeds and the announcement of Christ's Second Presence. This was unanimously rejected by the Protestant churches; and organized Protestant ecclesiasticism from 1878 on for forty years became the Judah of this type, besieged on every side by the reform element, under the leadership of the steward of Divine Truth, Pastor Russell. Until 1918, Hebrew reckoning, beginning in the fall of 1917, the civil powers continue as a 'wall of iron' protecting the Lord's people in their witness against error.[25]

With this exposition, Fisher provides confirmation that 1918 is to be the year that will see the destruction of Christendom, and much of the rest of his commentary supplies the details of that coming calamity. As Christendom totters, however, Zionism prospers:

'Thus saith the Lord God: I will also take of the highest branch of the high cedar, and will set it; I will crop off the top of his young twigs a tender one, and will plant it upon a high mountain and eminent.' [Ezekiel 17:22] Thus says the Lord God: One of the highest branches of ecclesiasticism is Judaism. I will establish Judaism. I will take, in Judaism, one of its young and tender aspirations – Zionism – and will plant it, establish it at the very pinnacle of the coming Kingdom of God – the Jews ruling, through the resurrected Ancient Worthies – Abraham, Isaac, Jacob, etc. – over the earthly phase of that Kingdom.[26]

Like Russell before him, Fisher saw in Ezekiel details of the final conflict which was to result in the establishment of Jerusalem as the capital of the earthly phase of the kingdom. But he also found an indication of when that was to happen. Ezekiel's vision of Jerusalem restored was given in the fourteenth year after the fall of the city (Ezekiel 40:1). Now, it has already been shown that the fall of the antitypical city was due in 1918; the fulfilment of the vision, then, by the establishment of the kingdom of God in Palestine can be expected during the fourteenth year after 1918, namely, 1931.[27] Then can be expected the assault upon Palestine which Russell had described in *The Battle of Armageddon* and to which he had assigned an earlier date.

This argument, though superficially similar to what has been used extensively before, nevertheless demonstrates a failure to appreciate the logic of the methods used in the construction of the system which is now being modified. Like Woodworth, whose treatment of Abraham's sacrifices misapplied the principles already established, Fisher had employed a method which has no prior justification. The argument has two major defects. First, the procedure which he had apparently sought to apply relates events to other events (not, strictly speaking, types and antitypes) but it had been used here to identify the period between a prophecy and its expected fulfilment. But, further, even if this is allowed, if it is intended to be modelled upon the argument from parallel dispensations, then it is being used in a way which is entirely novel. In Russell's hands the primary time indicator in this procedure was the location of a limited sequence of prophetically significant events within their own dispensation. So events at the close of the Jewish age prefigured their counterparts at the corresponding point in the close of the Gospel age. In each case there was a constant period of 1,845 years, the length of the Jewish and Gospel ages, between the prefiguring and the fulfilling events. It was only because this underlying relationship was established that it was legitimate to infer the period between fulfilling events from a corresponding period between prefiguring events. In Fisher's interpretation of Ezekiel 40:1 this underlying relationship clearly does not hold. The argument, therefore, is not consistent with the method upon which it is apparently based.

Observations

Though it was to be some years before the complete abandonment of Russell's system, *The Finished Mystery* marked a clear break with the past. It did, of course, represent the first acknowledgement that major revision was necessary but, more significantly, Woodworth's and Fisher's inability to match the standard of exposition which had been set by Russell was symptomatic of the separation from the millennialist tradition. From a distance, there is perhaps a tendency to regard all such doctrinal systems as equally eccentric. Close examination, however, reveals in Russell's work a degree of coherence and an appreciation of the underlying principles which is lacking in *The Finished Mystery*.

The Finished Mystery never achieved the status of a lastingly valid textbook which had been accorded to Russell's six volumes of *Studies in the Scriptures*. Having first been given a hostile reception by Rutherford's opponents within the movement, and having soon afterwards been banned in the United States of America and in Canada, it might have been expected to find its place during the years of reconstruction following the end of the First World War. Other literature, however, was to supersede it – and understandably so, for not only had Rutherford to consolidate his position as Russell's successor, but also some inconsistencies needed to be reconciled or otherwise eliminated. In particular there was the question of when the earthly phase of the kingdom was to begin. Woodworth looked forward to 1925, but Fisher identified 1931 as the crucial year. It will become clear in the next chapter that both proved to be significant years for the Watch Tower movement but for rather different reasons.

Notes

1. M. J. Penton, *Apocalypse Delayed*, pp. 44f.
2. A. O. Hudson, *Bible Students in Britain*, p. 93.
3. Penton, *op.cit.*, pp. 47ff. See also James A. Beckford, *The Trumpet of Prophecy*, pp. 22ff.
4. L. W. Jones, *What Pastor Russell Said*, p. 645.
5. *Ibid.*, p. 646.
6. Penton, *op.cit.*, pp. 55f.
7. C. T. Russell, *Thy Kingdom Come*, pp. 311ff.
8. C. J. Woodworth and G. Fisher (eds), *The Finished Mystery*, pp. 59f.
9. *Ibid.*, pp. 62f.
10. *Ibid.*, p. 64.
11. C. T. Russell, *The New Creation*, p. 93.

12. Woodworth and Fisher, *op. cit.*, p. 64.

13. *Ibid.*, p. 64.

14. *Ibid.*, p. 64.

15. C. T. Russell, *The Time is at Hand*, p. 266.

16. Woodworth and Fisher, *op. cit.*, p. 64.

17. Russell, *The Time is at Hand*, pp. 192ff.

18. Woodworth and Fisher, *op. cit.*, p. 128.

19. *Ibid.*, p. 301.

20. *Ibid.*, p. 386.

21. *Ibid.*, p. 563.

22. *Ibid.*, p. 128.

23. Woodworth's other contributions to this numerical exercise are an interpretation of the 'number of the beast' (Revelation 13:18) which relates it to the papal title, VICARIS FILII DEI, by adding up the Roman numerals found therein (p. 215); and the interpretation of the distance to which blood flowed from the wine press of God's anger (Revelation 14:20), as the distance between Brooklyn, New York, where *The Finished Mystery* was published and Scranton, Pennsylvania, where it was written (p. 230). Fisher finds in Ezekiel 1:1 a reference to Russell's age when he began to understand the prophecies of the Millennium (p. 367).

24. Woodworth and Fisher, *op. cit.*, p. 367.

25. *Ibid.*, pp. 393ff.

26. *Ibid.*, p. 450.

27. *Ibid.*, p. 569.

Chapter Twelve
Millions Now Living Will Never Die

The period during and immediately after the War proved to be a time of much difficulty for the Watch Tower movement. There was considerable disillusionment because of the failure of hopes in 1914, but recovery seemed to be well on the way by the time that Russell died in 1916. The change of leadership, however, created renewed difficulties as the subsiding disillusionment was rapidly followed by dissent caused by Rutherford's succession and his presidential style. The campaigning which provoked the arrest and imprisonment of the Society's directors brought ill feeling against the Bible Students generally and led to mob violence and discrimination against them, especially in the United States and Canada.[1] The effect of the movement's problems upon its numbers during this period is difficult to gauge because statistics are far from complete. Memorial attendance, however, for the years 1906 (6,267), 1911 (10,710) and 1917 (about 20,000) suggests that major losses may not have been experienced at first.[2] But losses were to come, as the decrease in subscriptions to *The Watch Tower and Herald of Christ's Presence* indicates. Before the First World War subscriptions to the magazine had risen to about 45,000; by its end the number of subscribers had fallen to fewer than 3,000.[3] The Bible Students, then, were an embattled and apparently diminishing community; instead of enjoying the blessings of the Millennium which they had confidently expected, they were in need of a new theology to handle their unexpected difficulties and to keep their hopes alive. *The Finished Mystery* had begun to supply that need but it was a confused and not easily readable book. Further work was called for.

Whether Rutherford recognised the deficiencies of *The Finished Mystery* it is possible only to surmise. He did, however, acknowledge the need for something more accessible than what was available at the end of the war[4] and began, at the first opportunity, to provide what was lacking. Following his release, he returned to a theme upon which he had lectured in California before his imprisonment, and began to indicate more clearly than had *The Finished Mystery* the direction which post-war revision was to take. In 1920 he embarked upon a major public speaking campaign and published a short book bearing the same title as his lecture: *Millions Now Living Will Never Die*. In it he developed a little further some of the ideas which had first been aired in Woodworth's contribution to *The Finished Mystery*, though he avoided the more obviously eccentric speculations. Referring to the same revised Jubilee calculation as before, Rutherford unambiguously identified 1925 as the start of the Millennium, the antitypical Jubilee:

> Seventy Jubilees of fifty years each would be a total of 3500 years. That period of time beginning 1575 before A.D. 1 of necessity would end in the fall of the year 1925, at which time the type ends and the great antitype begins. . . . Messiah's kingdom once established, Jesus and his glorified church constituting the great Messiah, shall minister the blessings to the people they have so long desired and hoped for and prayed might come. . . . We may confidently expect that 1925 will mark the return of Abraham, Isaac, Jacob and the faithful prophets of old.[5]

Because the Watch Tower Society for a long time acknowledged no responsibility for expectations raised by *Millions Now Living Will Never Die*, it is important to be clear what was explicitly forecast and what, though not explicit, was nevertheless implied.[6] First, the one definite prediction was that 1925 would see the resurrection of the 'ancient worthies'. Second, it is clear that Jerusalem was expected to be established as the seat of government of the kingdom of God on earth by that year: 'At that time the earthly phase of the kingdom shall be recognized.'[7] Rutherford's lack of detail concerning what this means, in comparison with Russell's very full description of the processes involved, reflects not a vagueness in this area of his doctrine but, rather, the more restricted format in which he had here chosen to express himself. There had been nothing at all yet to suggest any major revision of Russell's ideas other than, apparently, one of his dates; that being so, the details must continue to be supplied from *Studies in the Scriptures*.

The third expectation raised by *Millions Now Living Will Never Die* was the glorification of the last remaining members of the 'little flock'. Here, of course, the need for revision had been clear for some time, for the latest date which had been set for that, 1918, had passed without event. Rutherford, however, made no direct reference to when this was to be expected. The statement: 'Messiah's kingdom once established, Jesus and his glorified church . . . shall minister the blessings' could appear to leave room for the view that the completion of the glorified Church would come after the establishment of the kingdom. This, however, was to be a later amendment to Watch Tower thinking. Russell had believed that:

'The body of Christ,' will be glorified with the Head; because every member is to reign with Christ, being a joint-heir with him of the Kingdom, and it cannot be fully set up without every member.[8]

Rutherford was later to confirm that this remained his own view:

Following the glorification of the church and the making of the new covenant, Abraham, Isaac, Jacob, David, Barak, Jeptha, and the prophets . . . the Lord has promised shall be brought forth from the tomb.[9] (emphasis added)

1925, then, if it was to see the establishment of the earthly phase of the kingdom, would be the latest date for the glorification of the 'little flock'. For those who had expected to receive their heavenly reward first in 1878, then in 1881, then in 1914, and then in 1918, there could be no doubt that this meaning was intended.

The Harp of God

In 1921, Rutherford published *The Harp of God*, in which he carried a little further some of the ideas expressed in his earlier work – whose title, in fact, supplied the sub-title for the later book. In this book, though he appeared to be more cautious about the timing of events shortly to take place, he was by no means lacking in confidence in the details of those events. Although the revised Jubilee calculation and the year 1925 received no mention, his readers were left in no doubt about what was expected.

Rutherford continued to use Russell's end-time calendar, but with the addition of 1918 as the end of the Harvest and 1925 as the time for the establishment of the earthly phase of the kingdom. Although there are omissions, in *The Harp of God*, of certain dates from that calendar, it is perhaps premature to regard them as significant, especially in view of the fact that the reader is in several places referred to *Studies in the Scriptures* for a full treatment of the topic. However, the mere passage of time must bring with it some amendments. The beginning of a changed significance for 1914 has already been noted. Similarly, 1918 began to take on a new emphasis even before the theoretical basis for the new thinking was put forward. No longer could it be identified without qualification as the due time for the destruction of the churches of Christendom, even though it had seemed for a while that the suppression of the Church in Russia by the Bolshevik revolution had marked the beginning of Christendom's end.

So Rutherford identified 1918 only as the end of the Harvest of the Gospel age which was no longer seen as the time for the completion of all that remained to be done, for there was, following the Harvest, a gleaning work going on, in which a few Christians would be gathered in, as well as another part of the harvest work to be done.[10]

The end of Christendom was likewise prolonged:

> This gathering of the elements of Christendom, the vine of the earth, and the reaping of it for destruction, is now in progress.[11]

Whilst the reaping of Christendom and the gleaning continued, the faithful were not to expect a time of ease:

> No true Christian would expect to be without suffering or chastisements from the Lord, because these are evidences that he is a follower of Jesus and a son of God. It is one of the ways in which the spirit of the Lord testifies to us that we are his. (Hebrews 12:2-11; Romans 8:16,17) These sufferings of the Christian come from various agencies. The Christian suffers by being misunderstood. His motives are presumed to be wrong. He is sometimes charged with sedition because he does not desire to join with peoples of the world in engaging in war to destroy human lives; sometimes persecuted by false brethren, and sometimes by those who are ignorant. But all these afflictions he patiently endures, gladly.[12]

Such patience was soon to receive its reward:

> It is certain that the time must come when all those composing the body of Christ will have finished their course on this side of the vail (sic) and passed into heavenly glory; and since the Lord promised that his second presence would be for the purpose of gathering unto himself those who would compose his bride, we should expect the glorification of the church within a reasonably short time after the second presence of the Lord.[13]

Rutherford, then, encouraged the idea that the glorification of the Church was to occur in the immediate future. He even encouraged speculation concerning how it would be experienced:

> Since we are so close to that time, let us now assume in our minds that we are standing just beyond the vail (sic) and that we are getting the first glimpse of the glories of the kingdom.[14]

There follow four pages in which he attempted to describe the experience of the new arrival in the heavenly kingdom.

Following the glorification of the 'little flock', there begins the millennial restoration which is to bring mankind to perfection in a renewed paradise. Rutherford's treatment of this theme follows Russell but obviously places the work of restoration in a world recovering from the ravages of war.

1925 and After

If *Millions Now Living Will Never Die* and *The Harp of God* began to dispel some of the confusion which had been generated by *The Finished Mystery*, they did so only to a limited extent. A complete clarification, however, might not have been helpful at this stage. What, before 1925, was simply a degree of ambiguity about when the earthly phase of the kingdom was to be established may have provided, after the failure of hopes in 1925, some reason for continuing patience on the part of a minority at least of the Bible Students who were prepared to let developing world affairs determine the way in which the doctrine should be modified. The unambiguous rejection at too early a stage of 1931 as the due time for the inauguration of the kingdom could only have heightened the disillusionment of 1925. Nevertheless, 1931 had been virtually excluded from the system; it had been completely ignored in Rutherford's post-war campaign and, by 1926, a rift had developed between Rutherford and Fisher, the proponent of the later date.[15]

Despite the potential buffer which continuing uncertainty may have created, 1925 proved to be a major set-back for the Watch Tower movement. Unlike 1914, world affairs supplied nothing which could with hindsight be incorporated into the theory and, unlike the earlier date, it came at the end of the most difficult decade of the movement's history. Virtually the whole of the growth which had been experienced during the immediate post-war period was lost during the three years following 1925. Memorial attendance world-wide in 1920 was about 20,000; by 1925 the figure had risen to about 90,000, but by 1928 it had decreased to about 20,000.[16]

Notwithstanding the failure of 1925, Rutherford remained confident in the revised end-time calendar which he had put forward. There followed a few years during which he maintained a version of the ideas expressed in *Millions Now Living Will Never Die* and *The Harp of God* before abandoning them and beginning the construction of a completely new Watch Tower doctrine of the Millennium. Among his many publications after 1925 was the book, *Life*, which, in 1929, appeared at least as confident in the main features of the interim system as had the literature published prior to 1925. There are important differences between the version of that system expounded in *Life* and the version which appears in the earlier literature, but how much of the difference may be attributed to revision and how much to a change of emphasis or perspective, is by no means clear. Whatever the original motivation, however, the differences are noteworthy, for they help to chart the process whereby a completely new system was soon to emerge.

Rutherford's major preoccupation in *Life* was with the Jewish people. Not surprisingly, therefore, those elements of the end-time calendar which are of direct concern only to Christianity and Christendom receive no mention. So the question why the destruction of the churches had not taken place in 1918 is not addressed; a new reason to regard that date as significant is given. Without apparently intending to undermine Russell's identification of 1878 as the year when divine favour began to be restored to the Jewish people,

Rutherford identified 1918 as the time for the official re-establishment of the Jews in Palestine.[17] The supporting argument is identical to that offered in *The Finished Mystery*, that is, it is Russell's own revision of the argument from parallel dispensations based upon the observation that the end of the Jewish state in Judaea had taken place in AD 73. But where that argument had previously been used to shift the expected demise of Christendom from 1914 to 1918, it is now used to identify an event which had hitherto passed unnoticed, namely a major development in the establishment of the Jewish people in Palestine.

> It was in the spring of 1918 that Dr. Chaim Weizmann, clothed with an official commission from the British Empire, the mandatory over Palestine, opened offices in Jerusalem and began the laying of the foundation of the new Jewish government. Here, then, was the first official recognition; and it came exactly on time to fulfil the double, as pointed out by the foregoing prophecies.[18]

The event thus recognised is a new addition to the system but the support which is given is a relatively minor amendment to Russell's argument from parallel dispensations. It may seem at this stage, then, that there is no major break with the past.

1925 retained its place in the system with the same supporting argument as before, but where *Millions Now Living Will Never Die* had asserted that 'we may confidently expect that 1925 will mark the return of Abraham, Isaac, Jacob and the faithful prophets of old',[19] *Life* finds a rather different way in which the inauguration of the antitypical Jubilee was marked. The beginning of the typical Jubilee was announced by the sounding of a trumpet to inform the people that it had begun; the antitypical Jubilee likewise begins with proclamation:

> If the end of 1925 marks the end of the last fifty year period, then it follows that we should expect the people to begin to receive some knowledge concerning God's great plan of restoration. The Jews are to have the favors first, and thereafter all others who obey the Lord. There could be no restoration without knowledge, even as it is impossible to give a man anything unless he knows about it. A gift is a contract, and knowledge is the first and essential element on the part of both giver and receiver. From 1925 forward there has been the greatest proclamation of truth concerning Jehovah's government ever made on earth. That government means the restoration of man. The proclamation goes grandly on, and when that work is done restitution of the people must begin.[20]

Even though the Kingdom had not been established in Palestine as expected, Rutherford remained confident that events relating to the return of the Jews to their ancient homeland were in fulfilment of prophecy. Indeed, he found in the setting up of Zionism what he considered to be striking confirmation that it fulfilled Ezekiel's prophecy of the valley of the dry bones which came to life (Ezekiel 37).

> A human skeleton is made up of 206 bones. Zionism was organized into a body at Basel, Switzerland, in 1897; and in that congress, which perfected the organization, there were exactly 206 delegates, the same number as of bones that go to form the human body. That was not merely an accident, but a physical fact prearranged by the Lord, showing that God looks after the minutest things relative to the recovery of the Jews in bringing them back to himself.[21]

For Rutherford, if not for the majority of the Bible Students, there remained good reason for continuing confidence that the prophecies were in the course of fulfilment.

Also in 1929 Rutherford expressed confidence in his predictions in a more tangible way. Having acquired a plot of land at San Diego, California, he had built a large house which he named 'Beth Sarim'.

> The Hebrew words *Beth Sarim* mean 'House of the Princes'; and the purpose of acquiring that property and building the house was that there might be some tangible proof that there are those on earth today who fully believe God and Christ Jesus and in His kingdom, and who believe that the faithful men of old will soon be resurrected by the Lord, be back on earth, and take charge of the visible affairs of earth. The title to Beth Sarim is vested in the Watch Tower Bible and Tract Society in trust, to be used by the president of the Society and his assistants for the present, and thereafter to be forever at the disposal of the aforementioned princes on the earth.[22]

The great majority of Bible Students were unable to accept or even wait for the revisions to doctrine in the light of the failure of 1925 and by 1928 virtually the whole of the substantial post-war increase in numbers was lost. To what extent this massive disillusionment affected that core of the membership who had been with the movement from before the war, it is possible only to surmise. Nevertheless there seems to be no reason why such Bible Students should be any less susceptible to disillusionment than more recent converts. The loss of members during the years immediately following 1925, then, may represent one of the most significant of the movement's breaks with its early history.[23]

Other important breaks with the past were also to occur during this period. In 1927 what stocks remained of Russell's *Studies in the Scriptures* and of *The Finished Mystery* were disposed of and no further editions were published by the Society. Then, in 1931, at a convention held in Columbus, Ohio, the new name, 'Jehovah's Witnesses' was adopted, by which the Watch Tower Society clearly differentiated itself from the many independent groups of Bible Students which had seceded from the movement during the post-war years. Some of these have remained loyal to Russell's doctrines, whilst others, though continuing to hold Russell in much higher esteem than does the parent body, have allowed scope for some variation.

Observations

It is appropriate to pause at this stage to make a preliminary assessment of Rutherford's contribution to the Watch Tower doctrine of the Millennium. There are further major modifications to come, but by about the beginning of the 1930s the limit has been reached of that part of the process which may be described as adapting Russell's system. The amendments which were to follow amounted to the construction of a new and very different system.

Previously, when considering the emergence of Seventh-day Adventism and the Watch Tower movement from the disarray consequent upon the failure of Miller's expectations, it was possible to describe the relationship between those systems and their immediate predecessor in fairly straightforward terms. The Seventh-day Adventist system amounted basically to the redefinition of a single phrase, the 'cleansing of the sanctuary', which allowed the retention of Miller's system in full. Russell's system, on the other hand, though directly related, was a complete replacement of all that Miller had constructed. The subsequent development of Watch Tower millennialism exhibits something of both of these processes but it is far more complex.

To handle the complexities, it is useful to identify the range of basic ways in which millennialist systems may be adapted in response to the divergence between expectations and reality. The first possibility, which is hardly a modification at all, is *displacement*, whereby new areas of concern are brought to the fore and attention is diverted from potentially disillusioning scrutiny. The second possibility is *redefinition* of terms, whereby a system which had apparently failed can be retained with fulfilments matched to developing affairs rather than to original predictions. Thirdly, there is the bolder step of *reassignment* of expected events to different dates to produce a revised system. The fourth sort of response to perceived failure, of course, is *replacement* of one whole system by another. Finally, a millennialist system may be modified by *attrition*, or the unwitting loss of detail from otherwise unamended areas as modifications elsewhere, or simply the passage of time, force their own revisions.

In practice these processes may overlap or be combined. The rise of Seventh-day Adventism, for example, involved both redefinition, whereby Miller's system was rescued from dependence upon observable events in 1844, and displacement, which put new doctrines into central place. Russell's contribution was the replacement of Miller's system with his own, but redefinition played an important part, particularly as he substituted his own interpretation of the Second Presence of Christ.

Rutherford's amendments, during the early years of his presidency, of what had been inherited from Russell was, on the face of it, largely a matter of reassignment of developments which had been expected in 1914 to new dates. But this reassignment brought with it amendments by attrition. The end of the 'times of the Gentiles', though it had not been subjected to redefinition, could no longer be described in just the same terms as before. No longer did it involve the furthest limit of human governments, nor the demise of Christendom, nor the establishment of the earthly phase of the kingdom of God. Similarly the reassignment of the beginning of the Millennium to 1925 changed the way in which the beginning of Christ's Second Presence might be defined, although no actual redefinition had been put forward.

Other amendments to the system by attrition were the result of the passage of time and the increasing distance from the millennialist tradition. In particular, Russell's interpretation of the 1,290 days and the 2,300 days disappeared, without being redefined, from Rutherford's version. Russell's treatment of these two periods had incorporated within his system the clear acknowledgement of its place within the tradition, as the end of the 1,290 days in 1829 was marked by the beginning of Miller's movement and the end of the 2,300 days in 1846 saw the 'cleansing of the sanctuary', or the emergence of that group from which the Watch Tower movement was to develop. Although these dates continued to be implied in Rutherford's exposition of the 1,260 days and the 1,335 days, they were allowed to sink into obscurity.

By the early 1930s, then, Rutherford had made extensive amendments to Russell's system but the resulting body of doctrine no longer exhibited the same degree of internal coherence as the original. To restore some coherence, the process would have to be continued but it is not clear that there was any longer the possibility of further *ad hoc* amendment without further attrition. Those elements of the system which are allowed to be subjected to attrition, however, are the ones which threaten to cause the greatest difficulty, for, raising questions which the movement's leadership does not address, they invite general speculation which may undermine the cohesiveness of the movement as a whole. The way forward, then, must lie with a new but not entirely dissimilar system, or with an entirely new area of concern, or else with some combination of the two.

Notes

1. J. Beckford, *The Trumpet of Prophecy*, p. 29.
2. *Ibid.*, p.18. M. J. Penton, *Apocalypse Delayed*, p. 61.
3. Beckford, *op. cit.*, pp. 18, 24.
4. J. F. Rutherford, *The Harp of God*, p. 7.
5. J. F. Rutherford, *Millions Now Living Will Never Die*, pp.88ff.
6. In recent years the Society has been rather more open about past failures. See *Jehovah's Witnesses, Proclaimers of God's Kingdom*, pp. 631ff.

7. Rutherford, *Millions Now Living Will Never Die*, p. 89.

8. C. T. Russell, *The Time is at Hand*, p. 77.

9. Rutherford, *The Harp of God*, p. 328.

10. *Ibid.*, p. 236.

11. *Ibid.*, p. 249.

12. *Ibid.*, p. 291.

13. *Ibid.*, p. 301.

14. *Ibid.*, p. 303.

15. Fisher was seeking to have Rutherford, as an *ex-officio* elder of every ecelesia of the Bible Students, brought before each ecclesia on a disciplinary charge for having attended Al Jolson's show, *Artists and Models*, which was at that time widely regarded as a morally dubious entertainment. Fisher died, however, in July 1926 and his charges were never pursued. Penton, *op. cit.*, p. 318.

16. *Ibid.*, p.61.

17. J. F. Rutherford, *Life*, p. 154.

18. *Ibid.*, pp. 157f.

19. Rutherford, *Millions Now Living Will Never Die*, p. 89.

20. Rutherford, *Life*, p. 170.

21. *Ibid.*, pp. 177f.

22. J. F. Rutherford, *Salvation*, p. 311.

23. James Parkinson of Los Angeles, a historian of the Bible Student movement, has suggested to me in private correspondence that the defections in the wake of 1925 involved not only relative newcomers but also many members of long standing.

Chapter Thirteen
The Great Multitude

The adoption, in 1931, of the new name 'Jehovah's Witnesses' signalled a major break with the past. The next important step came in the spring of 1935 when Rutherford delivered a lecture to an assembly of Jehovah's Witnesses in Washington DC on the subject of the 'great multitude'[1] setting out what was to prove the basis for the movement's expansion during the following decades. The text of his lecture was published in *The Watchtower* in August of that year and the subject was further developed the following year in his book, *Riches*.

Although the expectation of the outbreak of Armageddon in the immediate future continued to characterise Watch Tower beliefs, it was at this point especially that the revised teachings began to make room for the possibility of an indeterminate extension of the Society's mission this side of Armageddon. That became a real possibility with the further loosening of the movement's attachment to its original end-time calendar.

> There was a measure of disappointment on the part of Jehovah's faithful ones on earth concerning the years 1914, 1918 and 1925, which disappointment lasted for a time. Later the faithful learned that these dates were definitely fixed in the Scriptures; and they learned also to quit fixing dates for the future and predicting what would come to pass on a certain date.[2]

The beginning of this process was the fairly subtle shift in the balance of emphasis from almost exclusive preoccupation with anticipated fulfilments to a greater concern with what remained to be accomplished before Armageddon. Along with that shift of emphasis, there was introduced the idea that the last remaining members of the 'little flock', instead of being removed from the earthly scene before the end, would first have the satisfaction of seeing their message vindicated.

> Jehovah has spoken his word and will perform it, and the Scriptures seem clearly to indicate that Jehovah will grant to his faithful witnesses the privilege of seeing his great 'act', thereby proving that his witnesses have spoken the truth according to his will, and that this he will do before his witnesses are 'changed' into the glorious organism like unto Christ Jesus.[3]

The new departure involved more than simply the removal of the glorification of the 'little flock' from the end-time calendar, where its location had proved continually troublesome; it also included the recognition of a hitherto unidentified transition which was to take one of the places in the calendar to which the 'little flock's' reward had previously been allocated. Russell had interpreted Elijah as a prophetic type of the 'little flock' and Elisha, his successor, as the type of a group which would come to prominence after the battle of Armageddon. Woodworth, in *The Finished Mystery*, had identified Elisha as a type of the 'great multitude' during the period between 1918 and 1921. Rutherford's new interpretation of these figures builds upon Russell's ideas but sets aside Woodworth's contribution. Writing in 1936, Rutherford described the work of Elijah as a type of the work undertaken by the faithful during the period from 1878 to 1918. Just as Elijah was succeeded after a short interval by Elisha, so in the modern period the Elijah work was superseded by a new work which, beginning in 1919, was typified by Elisha. In each case, the group so represented comprised the last remaining members, or remnant, of the 'little flock'.[4]

Other participants in the ancient drama were also treated as prophetic types. Jehu was assigned a complex reference:

He was a type or picture of Jehovah's elect servant and sometimes foreshadowed both Christ Jesus and his faithful followers.[5]

Though Jehu came to prominence during the career of Elisha, his prophetic significance began somewhat earlier:

Jehu came in contact with the prophet Elijah and lived for more than twenty-eight years of the period of the prophet Elisha. This appears to mean that Jehovah, during the Elijah period, that is, from A.D. 1878 to A.D. 1918, began to prepare a people to be witnesses to the name of Jehovah, and that those who prove faithful during that period were brought over into the Elisha period, which began in A.D. 1919, and that these are made members of God's organization.[6]

Jehu, then, was taken to represent the 'little flock' during the period following 1919, like Elisha; as a prophetic figure he illustrated the continuity with the earlier period but, more importantly, his role as executioner of Baal worshippers indicated that the due time for divine retribution against Christendom was imminent.

A particularly important figure in this drama, as it is related to the history of the Watch Tower movement, was Jonadab. As a Kenite he was a circumcised worshipper of Jehovah but not an Israelite; similarly, his role in the drama is that of the sympathetic and supportive observer but not the direct participant (2 Kings 10:15-29).

Jonadab represented or foreshadowed that class of people now on the earth during the time that the Jehu work is in progress who are of good will, are out of harmony with Satan's organization, take their stand on the side of righteousness, and are the ones whom, if obedient and faithful, the Lord will preserve during the time of Armageddon, take them through that trouble, and give them everlasting life on the earth.[7]

This is the same group of people elsewhere described as the 'great multitude' or the 'other sheep'. Where Russell had expected that these people would not be identified until after Armageddon, Rutherford began to bring them within his movement before. Russell, indeed, had asserted that none but members of the 'little flock' had sufficient light or influence of the Holy Spirit to be able to make their response until after Armageddon. For Rutherford, however, the Watch Tower movement, as Jehovah's organisation, was the antitype of the ancient cities of refuge, so it became essential for all who wished to survive Armageddon to attach themselves to that organisation.[8]

Along with the gathering of the Jonadabs or the 'great multitude' there came a very different view of the nature of the battle of Armageddon. Russell had seen that battle as the final eruption of chaos in an irreversibly disordered world. By means of that chaos God would bring about the destruction of all unrighteous institutions – but it was primarily the institutions, not the people, that were to be destroyed. Indeed, humanity would be rescued from destruction by divine intervention and the establishment of the earthly phase of the kingdom, and those who perished in the battle would be resurrected to be given their chance to take their stand for righteousness.

Perhaps one of the causes of the harsher picture of Armageddon was the rough treatment during and after the First World War of the Bible Students at the hands of Church, state and the general populace. A further factor may have been the prolonged delay of Armageddon, which allowed an extension of the preaching work not previously envisaged. When Armageddon did eventually begin, Rutherford came to believe, none who had by that time failed to identify themselves as being within Jehovah's organisation could expect to be spared.[9]

This hardened attitude gave to the preaching work a new urgency and impetus as the Witnesses accepted responsibility for warning the world of what was to come. Under Russell's regime, the function of the preaching had been to enable those called to be members of the 'little flock' to make good their calling. It was only with Rutherford's doctrine of the Jonadabs that there came the necessity to provide real opportunities for all to make the informed choice which had not hitherto been expected of any except the 'little flock' until after Armageddon. Further, as the vast majority of mankind were virtually written off by Rutherford, and the Jonadabs identified as the only expected survivors of Armageddon, along with a small remnant of the 'little flock', it was natural that Rutherford should do away with Russell's identification of two heavenly classes, the 'little flock' and the 'great multitude'. The latter group were now assigned an earthly reward.[10]

From the beginning, the new doctrine of the 'great multitude' laid emphasis upon the responsibility to participate in mission:

> The people of good will on the earth today who hear the truth do not
> remain mum, but vigorously join Jehovah's witnesses, the remnant,
> in crying out the Kingdom message.[11]

This was in marked contrast with the earlier view of a class of sympathetic adherents who, though welcome to join in mission alongside the 'little flock', were not required to do so. Nevertheless, a thoroughgoing distinction between the two bodies remained and was reflected in the fact that at first the name Jehovah's Witnesses was applied only to members of the 'little flock'. As the movement grew and this body dwindled, it was natural that in due course the name should embrace the whole membership, and that the role of Jonadab as a sympathetic observer but not an active participant, which may not have helped Rutherford's intention to mobilise the 'great multitude' for mission, should be allowed to disappear from view.

The doctrine of the 'great multitude', then, supplied a vitally important theological explanation of the continued delay of Armageddon. In this respect it served a similar purpose to the Adventist interpretation of the parable of the wise and foolish virgins, but where that parable had merely signalled unexpected delay and the need for patient waiting, Rutherford's new doctrine identified a major task to be undertaken during the time of waiting as the old world limped on to its end, and implied some considerable delay before the onset of Armageddon. A further strength of the new teaching, during the transitional period, lay in the fact that it did not directly challenge the old view of the Harvest, for that had centred upon the 'little flock'. Indeed, the 'great multitude, as it was now defined', could not begin to be formed until after the end of the Harvest.[12] The practical importance of the doctrine is well demonstrated by the massive expansion of the Watch Tower movement after it had emerged from the difficulties of the late 1920s. In 1928, worldwide attendance at the Memorial had been about 20,000, the majority of whom would have considered themselves to be members of the 'little flock'. In 1992, Memorial attendance was over 11,000,000, of whom only 8,683 partook of the bread and wine, thereby claiming for themselves membership of the 'little flock'.[13]

The Emergence of a New Doctrine of the Kingdom
With the passage of time, any predictive system must undergo change; there must come an accumulation of greater detail in the historical component of the system and a corresponding reduction in the predictive component. In the most straightforward case, yesterday's forecast becomes today's report. In the least satisfactory case, by contrast, the balance of detail between the two parts remains the same as unfulfilled expectations are continually deferred. The two extremes, however, do not exhaust the possibilities. It has already been observed that developing events may be allowed to redefine predictions, as happened in the case of the Seventh-day Adventist understanding of the cleansing of the sanctuary, and as was implicit in the later Watch Tower understanding of the end of the 'times of the Gentiles'. But further, the exposition of the prophetic corpus in the light of developing events may begin to treat areas which had previously received little or no attention and which had not, therefore, generated any predictions. Rutherford's treatment of Elijah, Elisha, Jehu and Jonadab is an example of this process.

As this development proceeds, the nature of supporting argument changes. So long as fulfilment is mostly in the future, the main question to be addressed is why events may be expected at the dates assigned. As more and more prophecy is said to have been fulfilled, the main concern becomes why it should be believed that particular events fulfil particular prophecies. The perceived validity of the whole process, then, comes to depend upon whether such questions receive satisfactory answers, rather than upon the original reasons for believing the predictions. The result, in the case of the Watch Tower movement, has been a body of doctrine in which the chronological approach that characterised the early years has come to occupy a position of reduced importance and its amendment has been pursued with less rigour than the descriptive element which charts the fulfilment of prophecy since 1914. What remains is a hybrid system in which the historical or descriptive element is almost entirely new, whereas the chronological supportive arguments are an adaptation of what was left after the bulk of the chronology had been discarded.

By the time that the new teaching regarding the 'great multitude' was brought in, there had been significant development in the doctrine of the 'time of the end' and the kingdom of God. The result was a body of doctrine which marked the end of the period of greatest uncertainty and secured the movement's future, but in doing so it created a system which bore only superficial resemblance to that which Russell had espoused.

The hardening of attitudes toward those outside the Watch Tower movement, which has already been noted, drew its impetus not only from the Society's experiences of persecution during and after the First World War, but also from a doctrinal foundation in the new ideas that Rutherford was bringing forward. Where Russell had defined his movement's mission in terms of the calling of the 'little flock', and Armageddon in terms of God's intervention in the final chaos of a sinful world, Rutherford related both to the ages-long struggle between Satan and his organisation on the one hand, and Jehovah and his organisation on the other hand.

This provided a new description of what had taken place in 1914. It was then, at the end of the 'times of the Gentiles', that Christ had been enthroned in heaven as King and his second presence began, and what followed fulfilled one of the visions of Revelation:

> And there was war in heaven: Michael and his angels fought against the dragon; and the dragon fought and his angels, and prevailed not; neither was their place found any more in heaven. And the great dragon was cast out, that old serpent, called the Devil, and Satan, which deceiveth the whole world: he was cast out into the earth and his angels were cast out with him. . . . Therefore rejoice, ye heavens, and ye that dwell in them. Woe to the inhabiters of the earth and of the sea! For the devil is come down unto you, having great wrath, because he knoweth that he hath but a short time. (Revelation 12:7-12)

So the first action of the newly enthroned Christ, signified here by Michael, was to rid heaven of Satan and his demons. The consequence for human society, to which Satan's activities have since been confined, was the outbreak of war in 1914 and the continuing troubles thereafter.[14]

This interpretation of events implies a radical change in what is meant by the end of the 'times of the Gentiles'. The end of 2,520 years during which the typical kingdom of God was 'trodden down of the Gentiles' (Luke 21:24), was marked, not by the re-establishment of an earthly, Jewish kingdom, but by the inauguration of the great heavenly antitype. The new teaching obviously called for a reappraisal of the place of the Jewish people in the divine plan. This came in 1932 with the publication of *Vindication*, the second volume of which put forward Rutherford's new belief that those prophecies of Ezekiel which had seemed to indicate restored fortunes for Israel at the 'time of the end' referred not to fleshly Israel but to spiritual Israel which is the 'little flock' of Jehovah's Witnesses.[15]

The removal of fleshly Israel from the end-time fulfilments required some adjustment in the chronology of the 'times of the Gentiles'. Russell, it will be remembered, had found two indications of this period: Leviticus 26 pointed to a period of 2,520 years between the exile in Babylon and the restoration of the Jewish people to divine favour in 1914; and Daniel 4 showed that, in parallel with this, there was to be a corresponding period of degradation for humanity in general. The new derivation of the 'times of the Gentiles' abandoned Leviticus and revised the understanding of Daniel. The symbolism of that vision now seems to have a composite reference. First, the tree refers to Nebuchadnezzar and the seven years during which it is restrained from growth have their fulfilment in his seven years of madness. Secondly:

> In this drama Jehovah used the king of Babylon to picture a yet greater fulfillment of the prophecy, namely, the cutting down of the unfaithful cherub from his position in Eden and the later reinstatement of theocratic rule over earth.[16]

Thirdly, the tree is also understood to symbolise the kingdom of God which, as the typical Jewish kingdom, came to an end in 607 BC and which flourished once more with the establishment of the antitypical kingdom in 1914.[17]

The difficulty with the second level of meaning noted above, of course, is that the period between the demise of the cherub in Eden and 1914 is very much more than 'seven times', and it is, perhaps, for this reason that this understanding has been allowed to disappear from view in the more recent literature. What remains has the appearance of a traditional interpretation of prophecy in which a minor fulfilment becomes the type of a major fulfilment. However, I think it would be unfair to press this to the point where the king of Babylon must be seen as a type of the kingdom of God, which in Watch Tower theology is a clear absurdity. Indeed, a more recent treatment of this vision seems to suggest that the minor fulfilment in Nebuchadnezzar is to be regarded, not as typical of the major fulfilment, but rather as adding a further detail to the vision. So, the tree represents theocracy, or the kingdom of God, which is in abeyance for 'seven times', and Nebuchadnezzar's madness represents the condition of the world powers which are dominant during that period.[18] Nevertheless, his restoration to sanity and the throne seems either to have no counterpart in the fulfilment at the end of the 'times of the Gentiles', or else suggests that he does, after all, typify the kingdom of God.

The dismantling of Russell's system was completed in 1943 with the publication of *The Truth Shall Make You Free*, in which the hitherto accepted chronology of the Old Testament period was adjusted. Following a suggestion by Benjamin Wilson, a Christadelphian Bible translator, Russell had assumed that 1 Kings 6:1, which gave the period between the exodus and the building of the first temple as 480 years, contained an error of transcription and that the period was, in fact, 580 years.[19] In 1943 it was accepted that no such error had occurred.[20] The effect of this revision was to shorten the Jewish age by one century and consequently, at a time when, if anything, the Gospel age needed to be lengthened rather than shortened, to remove all possibility of any reworking of Russell's argument from parallel dispensations.

The traditional historicist component of Russell's system was likewise made no longer tenable because the major events which had derived support from that approach, that is, the beginning of the Second Presence of Christ and the beginning of the Millennium, were reassigned. Accordingly the 1,260, 1,290, 1,335, and 2,300 days of Daniel's vision required to be given new interpretations, but the mere passage of time rendered unlikely any plausible new application of the year-for-a-day principle. Naturally, then, the periods came to be treated as literal, but not completely so. In each case the period is converted to years and months on the basis of the 360-day year of the historicist tradition, but in the application the number of years thus calculated is always treated as that many ordinary calendar years. The result is that the periods are all lengthened, the whole sequence being extended by some eighty days. Chapter 14 will take a closer look at the significance of these periods in current Watch Tower chronology.

A Picture of the 'Last Days'

Christ's enthronement in heaven in 1914 set in train a sequence of events which was expected to reach its climax at the battle of Armageddon in the near future. Satan's defeat and confinement to the earth that year were the direct cause of the outbreak of the First World War, which, if not quite the time of trouble about which Russell and the Bible Students had been giving warning for nearly forty years, was nevertheless taken as confirmation that all was being fulfilled according to the divine schedule. Immediate blessings for the Bible Students did not follow but, in due course, they came to believe that the difficulties which they experienced during those years had been prophesied and were, indeed, no setback at all.

The general pattern of events of the 'last days' is represented symbolically in Revelation, beginning at chapter 6. As each of seven seals on a scroll (Revelation 5:5) is opened, the overall picture is gradually revealed.

And I saw when the Lamb opened one of the seven seals, and I heard one of the four living creatures say with a voice as of thunder: 'Come!' And I saw, and, look! a white horse; and the one seated upon it had a bow; and a crown was given to him, and he went forth conquering. (Revelation 6:1,2)[21]

The rider on the white horse is Christ and the vision indicates that his enthronement inaugurates a time of conquest. This began, as has already been noted, with the conquest and abasement of Satan.

Jesus' ride of conquest continues through the opening decades of the Lord's day while the nations and peoples of earth are being judged and sheeplike humans are being gathered to the King's side for salvation. . . . What other conquests has Jesus made during the past 70-and-more years of the Lord's day? Around the globe, individually and as a congregation, Jehovah's people have experienced many hardships, pressures and persecutions. . . . Jesus conquered on their behalf. And he will continue to go forth conquering in our behalf, as long as we are resolved to complete our conquest of faith. – 1 John 5:4. The global congregation of Jehovah's Witnesses has shared in many conquests under the guidance of its conquering King. Outstandingly, he protected the Bible Students from annihilation in 1918, when they themselves were 'conquered' temporarily by Satan's political organization. In 1919, however, he broke prison bars to rescue them and he enlivened them to proclaim the good news 'to the most distant part of the earth.' – Revelation 13:7; Acts 1:8.[22]

Jesus' conquering ride during the 'last days', then, begins with the initial defeat of Satan, continues with the rescue or protection of his people from harm, and will culminate in victory against Satan's entire organiszation at Armageddon.

In response to the opening of the second seal,

Another came forth, a fiery-colored horse; and to the one seated upon it there was granted to take peace away from the earth so that they should slaughter one another; and a great sword was given him. (Revelation 6:4)

What is represented here, by contrast with the righteous warfare of Christ, is the human warfare which has marked the 'last days' ever since the outbreak of the First World War, together with the development of increasingly destructive weaponry. A frequent consequence of war, especially during the 'last days', is famine, which is signified with the opening of the third scroll, when there appeared,

a black horse; and the one seated upon it had a pair of scales in his hand. (Revelation 6:5)[23]

The opening of the fourth seal revealed another rider:

And I saw, and, look! a pale horse; and the one seated upon it had the name Death. And Hades was closely following him. (Revelation 6:8)

This warns of widespread disease during the decades leading up to Armageddon and has had its fulfilment from the outbreak of Spanish flu in the aftermath of the First World War to the worldwide plague of AIDS today. With the opening of the fifth seal the focus of attention changes from the earthly scene to the heavenly:

And when he opened the fifth seal, I saw underneath the altar the souls of those slaughtered because of the word of God and because of the witness work that they used to have. And they cried with a loud voice, saying: 'Until when, Sovereign Lord holy and true, are you refraining from judging and avenging our blood upon those who dwell upon the earth?' (Revelation 6:9,10)

The reference, in its more nearly literal sense, is to Christians who suffered martyrdom. But, more generally, it applies to all members of the 'little flock'.

Indeed, all those who are begotten as spirit sons of God die a sacrificial death. Because of the role they are to play in Jehovah's heavenly Kingdom, it is God's will that they renounce and sacrifice any hope of life everlasting on earth. In this respect they submit to a sacrificial death in behalf of Jehovah's sovereignty.[24]

And a white robe was given to each of them; and they were told to rest a little while longer, until the number was filled also of their fellow slaves and their brothers who were about to be killed as they also had been. (Revelation 6:11)

The white robes signify resurrection; the fact that those who are resurrected at this point are told they must wait until the full number is completed indicates that the resurrection of the dead in Christ is to begin whilst a remnant of the 'little flock' is still on earth.

> All the evidence indicates that this heavenly resurrection began in 1918, after Jesus' enthronement in 1914 and his riding forth to start his kingly conquest of Satan and his demons. . . . Their rest will end when they witness the destruction of false religion and, as 'called and chosen and faithful' ones, they accompany the Lord Jesus Christ in executing judgement on all other parts of Satan's wicked seed here on earth.[25]

The opening of the sixth seal reveals one of the pictures of the eventual climax:

> And I saw when he opened the sixth seal, and a great earthquake occurred. And the sun became black as sackcloth of hair, and the entire moon became as blood, and the stars of heaven fell to the earth, as when a fig tree shaken by a high wind casts its unripe figs. (Revelation 6:12,13)

Though literal earthquakes since 1914 fulfil the prophecy, they are of minor significance; more important is the symbolic fulfilment which comes as

> the devastating *finale* to a series of advance tremors that shake Satan's human earthly system of things to its foundation.[26]

This shaking of Satan's visible organisation began immediately following the end of the 'times of the Gentiles' in 1914. It has resulted in political and economic instability and has been marked especially by events such as the Bolshevik Revolution of 1917, the stock market crash of 1929, the rise of Nazism and the Second World War. It will reach its climax in,

> the great earthquake in which all humans opposed to Jehovah God's sovereignty are destroyed. . . . When the great earthquake strikes, this entire world system will be engulfed in the despair of total darkness. The bright, shining luminaries of Satan's earthly system will send forth no ray of hope.[27]

The great earthquake, however, does not lead immediately to indiscriminate destruction. Revelation 7:1-8 speaks of four angels who hold back the winds of destruction in order that the faithful may be saved. First, the 'little flock', which is shown here to comprise 144,000 members, is sealed, and then the 'great crowd' is identified. Once the faithful are taken care of, it appears, the end can come, so the chapter closes with words which are echoed in the final chapters of the book:

> They will hunger no more nor thirst anymore, neither will the sun beat down upon them now any scorching heat, because the Lamb, who is in the midst of the throne, will shepherd them, and will guide them to fountains of waters of life. And God will wipe out every tear from their eyes. (Revelation 7:16, 17)

The picture of the 'last days,' however, is not complete; the breaking of the seventh seal introduces a further set of revelations which add to what has already been given.

Notes

1. The terms 'great company', 'great multitude' and 'great crowd', which derive from Revelation 7:9, are synonymous and were used at different periods, reflecting the translation of the Bible favoured at the time.
2. J. F. Rutherford, *Vindication*, pp. 338f.
3. *Ibid.*, p. 339.
4. J. F. Rutherford, *Riches*, pp. 66f.
5. *Ibid.*, p. 67.
6. *Ibid.*, pp. 67f.
7. *Ibid.*, p. 78.
8. *Ibid.*, p. 123.
9. *Ibid.*, p. 98.
10. *Ibid.*, p. 294.
11. *Ibid.*, p. 300.
12. *Ibid.*, p. 308.
13. *The Watchtower*, 1 January 1993, p. 15.
14. J. F. Rutherford, *Light*, Book 1, pp. 236ff.
15. Anon., *God's Kingdom of a Thousand Years Has Approached*, p. 266.
16. Anon., *Let God Be True* (1952 edition), p. 251.
17. *Ibid.*, p. 253.
18. Anon., *Babylon the Great has Fallen*, pp. 174ff.
19. C. T. Russell, *The Time is at Hand*, p.53. See also B. Wilson, *The Emphatic Diaglott* (1942 edition), p. 449.
20. Anon., *God's Kingdom of a Thousand Years Has Approached*, p. 209.
21. From this point onwards, all Scripture quotations are from the *New World Translation of the Holy Scriptures*, 1984 edition, unless otherwise indicated.
22. Anon., *Revelation – Its Grand Climax at Hand*, pp. 90f.
23. *Ibid.*, pp. 94ff.
24. *Ibid.*, p. 100.
25. *Ibid.*, p. 103.
26. *Ibid.*, p. 105.
27. *Ibid.*, pp. 109f.

Chapter Fourteen

Interpreting the Current Sources

One of the difficulties which is encountered when attempting to provide a systematic description of current Watch Tower millennialism arises from the fact that the Society's own treatment of the subject proceeds in an *ad hoc* manner. The difficulty is greatest when considering the movement's theological explanation of its troubles during the First World War and the recovery thereafter, a topic which is at the heart of the Society's ecclesiology.

The most important modern sources are a number of books published since 1958 from which the overall doctrine may be put together.[1] However, it has long been the practice of the Society, where revision of doctrine has been found to be necessary, to publish an up-to-date treatment superseding the earlier position, but this has often been done without explicit reference to what has been superseded. This situation is further complicated by the fact that since the beginning of Nathan Knorr's presidency in 1942 all the literature has been published anonymously. Some information concerning authorship is available but it is not possible to make a complete assessment of the extent to which differences of doctrinal treatment may reflect the respective points of view of different writers or teams of writers. Since it has always been the Society's intention that variation of this sort should not occur, it is, perhaps, fair to assume that where there are significant differences of treatment, a later publication is always intended to supersede an earlier one. Much of the time, no confusion arises. In the case of Watch Tower ecclesiology especially, however, there may be some variation remaining in what has so far been published which cannot be resolved by assuming that the later treatment supersedes the earlier. So, whilst one ought not portray as confused what may be capable of coherent explanation, some caution must be exercised when offering solutions to problems which have not been addressed. With that *caveat* the history of the 'last days' is resumed, and where it is not clear how, or whether, the Society would resolve some apparent discrepancies which have appeared in the literature, the alternative interpretations will be set out.

Silence in Heaven

The opening of the six seals gradually revealed a general picture of the 'last days'. With the opening of the seventh seal, attention returns to the beginning

of that period and important details are added to what has already been given.
And when he opened the seventh seal, a silence occurred in heaven
for about half an hour. And I saw the seven angels that stand before
God, and seven trumpets were given them. And another angel arrived
and stood at the altar, having a golden incense vessel; and a large
quantity of incense was given him to offer it with the prayers of all the
holy ones upon the golden altar that was before the throne. And the
smoke of the incense ascended from the hand of the angel with the
prayers of the holy ones before God. (Revelation 8:1-4)

The most recent commentary on these verses illustrates the way in which
much Watch Tower interpretation of prophecy now proceeds:

Under the Jewish system of things, incense was burned daily. . . . John
now sees something similar happening in heaven. The incense offered
by the angel is associated with 'the prayers of the holy ones.' In fact,
in an earlier vision, incense is said to represent such prayers.
(Revelation 5:8; Psalm 14:1, 2) Evidently, then, the symbolic silence
in heaven is to allow the prayers of the holy ones on earth to be heard.
Can we determine when this happened? Yes, we can. . . . During 1918
and 1919, events on earth harmonized remarkably with the scenario
described at Revelation 8:1-4. For 40 years before 1914, the Bible
Students – as Jehovah's Witnesses were then called – had been
announcing boldly that the times of the Gentiles would end in that
year. The distressful events of 1914 proved them correct. (Luke 21:24,
King James Version; Matthew 24:3,7,8) But many of them also
believed that in 1914 they would be taken from this earth to their
heavenly inheritance. That did not happen. Instead, during the first
world war, they endured a time of severe persecution. On October 31,
1916, the first president of the Watch Tower Society, Charles T. Russell,
died. Then, on July 4, 1918, the new president, Joseph F. Rutherford,
and seven other representatives of the Society were transported to
Atlanta, Georgia, penitentiary, wrongly sentenced to long years in
prison. . . . An article entitled 'The Harvest Ended – What Shall
Follow?' appeared in the May 1, 1919, issue of *The Watch Tower*. It
reflected this state of uncertainty and encouraged the faithful to
continued endurance, adding: 'We believe it is now a true saying that
the harvest of the kingdom class is an accomplished fact, that all such
are duly sealed and that the door is closed.' During this difficult period,
the fervent prayers of the John class were ascending, as though in the
smoke of a large quantity of incense. And their prayers were being
heard![2]

An important point to note here is the absence of external supporting argument,
by which is meant the kind of argument which seeks to establish the time at
which the prophecies became due for fulfilment and which, in principle at
least, could have been deployed in advance. Whereas Russell's end-time
calendar had been underpinned by an array of such arguments, little of the
kind is to be found in today's Watch Tower doctrine of the 'last days'. Much
depends upon accepting that 1914 has been proven to be the end of the 'times
of the Gentiles'; thereafter the procedure appears to be to match events to the

prophecies in order to determine the best correspondence between the two. So, given that it was in 1914 that the visions of Revelation began to have their fulfilment, it seems reasonable to suppose that the end of the War had some connection with the holding back of the four winds of destruction and that the few months thereafter, when the Society's future was most in doubt, should be represented in the vision by the half hour of silence in heaven whilst the prayers of the faithful were heard. So long as it is possible to interpret the rest of the prophetic corpus in like manner, the resulting body of doctrine may appear persuasive.

The procedure at this point is, on the face of it, similar to that followed in the interpretation of the six seals. However, the direction of dependence is reversed. The general conditions described in the exegesis of Revelation 6 lend support to the contention that the kingdom was established in heaven in 1914. So if it is asked how 1914 may be identified as the crucial date, then the apparent fulfilment of Revelation 6 (and Matthew 24 and parallels) may be offered as evidence instead of the external line of argument noted above. Conversely, however, if the experience of the Watch Tower movement during the months following the end of the First World War is to be seen as a fulfilment of Revelation 8, it requires first that the place of 1914 in the system be established. Unless 1914 is first secured, the argument that events immediately following the First World War fulfilled Revelation 8 loses its force. Similar lines of dependence may be observed throughout the whole body of doctrine. The result is a system in which the individual elements may each seem to draw strong support from the rest of the system, whilst the whole is dependent upon a single external argument.

If the opening verses of Revelation 8 describes the prayers of the Bible Students between 1918 and 1919, the rest of the chapter describes the outcome:

> But right away the angel took the incense vessel, and he filled it with some of the fire of the altar and hurled it to the earth. And thunders occurred and voices and lightnings and an earthquake. (Revelation 8:5)

This verse began to have its fulfilment in 1919 when, following the release of the Society's directors, the activity of the Bible Students was revived.

> In September of that year, Jehovah's spirit was remarkably in evidence as his loyal Witnesses assembled from near and far at Cedar Point, Ohio, U.S.A. Joseph F. Rutherford, recently released from prison and soon to be completely exonerated, boldly addressed that convention, saying: 'Obedient to the command of our Master, and recognizing our privilege and duty to make war against the strongholds of error which have so long held the people in bondage, our vocation was and is to announce the incoming glorious kingdom of Messiah.' . . . Fire was hurled to the earth in that God's Kingdom was made the burning issue, and so it continues to be![3]

Captivity and Release

The liberation of the Watch Tower movement in 1919 came in consequence of an earlier event of prophetic significance.

> Besides woe for the enemy nations, the finishing of the 'mystery of God' ushers in the 'appointed time for the dead to be judged, and to

give their reward to your slaves the prophets and to the holy ones and to those fearing your name, the small and the great.' (Revelation 11:18) That means resurrection from the dead!

But when? Not accidentally, the time of the ministry of Jesus Christ from his baptism in water to his resurrection from the dead corresponds with 'forty-two months,' or a 'thousand two hundred and sixty days,' from about Tishri 15 of the year 29 C.E. (Daniel 9:24-27) Just six days before his resurrection, or on Monday, Nisan 10, Jesus entered into the temple at Jerusalem and executed God's judgement there by cleansing the temple of those doing commercial business and making money there. (Matthew 21:12,13; Mark 11:11,15-17) In a similar manner, forty-two months or a thousand two hundred and sixty days from the end of the Gentile Times in 1914 C.E., the glorified Jesus accompanied his heavenly Father Jehovah God to the spiritual temple to start a judgement work.[4]

The spring of 1918, then, was when the dead in Christ were resurrected and judgement began for all professing Christians still on earth.

The 1,260 days of Revelation 11 (but not the similar period in chapter 12, which is applied differently) are thus identified with the three-and-a-half times of Daniel 7 and 12. They are further identified with the first half of the seventieth week of Daniel 9. This retains an echo of Russell's system in which the timing of significant events in the end-time calendar reflected the timing of corresponding events during Jesus' earthly ministry which had been indicated in the prophecy of the seventy weeks, but it lacks the justification of the argument from parallel dispensations.

During the 1,260 days from 1914 to 1918, the faithful were to prophesy dressed in sackcloth (Revelation 11:3). This has been explained in two rather different ways. In 1958 the book *Your Will Be Done on Earth* offered what may seem to be a natural explanation in view of the movement's disappointed hopes and the adversity which they faced, that prophesying in sackcloth represented the mournful condition of the Bible Students during the period up to 7 May 1918.[5] In 1969 there came an explicit revision:

This has been explained to designate the period from the first half of November of 1914 down till May 7, 1918. This explanation has been given because the 1,260 days were understood to refer to a period of self-centred, personal mourning on the part of the anointed remnant, sackcloth being a symbol of mourning during a black period. . . . However, the being dressed in sackcloth may not refer to private personal mourning because of disappointment of one's hopes and aspirations. Rather, it may refer to the nature of the prophecy that 'my two witnesses' prophesy. . . . During this period of time [5 October 1914 to 27 March 1918] they proclaimed a gloomy, mournful message for the nations.[6]

On each interpretation, the 1,260 days reach their climax not with the end of the movement's troubles, but with the intensification of that adversity.

And when they have finished their witnessing, the wild beast that ascends out of the abyss will make war with them and conquer them and kill them. . . . And those of the peoples and tribes and tongues and nations will look at their corpses for three and a half days. (Revelation 11:7-9)

This had its fulfilment when the arrest and imprisonment of the Society's leaders in May 1918 led to the almost complete cessation of the Bible Students' activities. Restored fortunes, however, were not far away:

> 'And after the three and a half days spirit of life from God entered into them, and they stood upon their feet, and great fear fell upon those beholding them. And they heard a loud voice out of heaven say to them: "Come on up here." And they went up into heaven in the cloud, and their enemies beheld them.' (Revelation 11:11, 12) Thus they had an experience similar to that of the dry bones in the valley that Ezekiel visited in vision. Jehovah breathed upon those dry bones, and they came to life, providing a picture of the rebirth of the nation of Israel after 70 years of captivity in Babylon. (Ezekiel 37:1-14) These two prophecies, in Ezekiel and in Revelation, had their striking modern-day fulfillment in 1919, when Jehovah restored his 'deceased' witnesses to vibrant life.[7]

In 1971 the Society described their 1919 revival as the commissioning of a latter-day prophet:

> Back there in the postwar year of 1919 there were none among the war-guilty religious elements of Jewry and Christendom who qualified to be commissioned as the modern-day counterpart or antitype of Ezekiel. . . . Whom could the real 'chariot' of Jehovah's organisation roll up to and confront that He might bestow upon this qualified one the commission to speak as a prophet in the name of Jehovah? Ah, there was a group whose members had suffered religious persecution during World War I at the hands of Babylon the Great, the world empire of false religion, and whose members had, in fact, come out of the religious organisations of Babylon the Great. In fact, they had refused to be a party with Christendom and with all the rest of Babylon the Great in actively taking part in carnal warfare during World War I.
>
> . . . It is manifest that in the year 1919 the invisible heavenly organisation of Jehovah, like the celestial chariot seen in Ezekiel's vision, rolled up and stopped, not before Christendom's advocates of the League of Nations, but before the anointed proclaimers of the heavenly kingdom of God. . . . Jehovah commissioned this dedicated, baptized, anointed class of servants to speak to all the nations in his name.[8]

The foregoing account, in which the Bible Students are depicted as martyred and vindicated, occupies a central place in the Watch Tower movement's understanding of itself. It is not, however, the only picture of this difficult period. Although the idea of the movement's experience during the war years as a 'Babylonish captivity' is a recurrent motif in Watch Tower literature, the related idea of chastisement and restoration to divine favour has only once been extensively treated in recent years. This occurred in 1975 with the publication of *Man's Salvation out of World Distress at Hand*. Although this book, like all other Watch Tower literature dealing with the subject, places the major responsibility for the movement's troubles between 1914 and 1919 upon Christendom, unlike the rest of the literature *Man's Salvation* identifies the Bible Students' own failings as a significant factor.

It was after the exiled Jews returned from Babylon in 537 B.C.E. that the prophecy of the beautification of the Judean 'wilderness,' 'waterless region' and 'desert' had a miniature fulfillment. The larger and final fulfillment, began to take place upon the remnant of spiritual Israelites after they returned from their exile from God's favor in Babylon the Great in the year 1919 C.E. Besides suffering the ill effects of the religious and political influence of Babylon the Great prior to the first world war, the spiritual estate of the spiritual Israelites was reduced to a desolate wilderness and desert by World War I. . . . During World War I the lack of rainfall of God's blessings and expressed approval had resulted in parched, unproductive areas in their privileges and the carrying out of their spiritual obligations to Jehovah God. He was in no position to bless the measure of fear of men that they displayed and the religious restraints that this imposed upon them. He could not bless the measure of contamination with the warring world with which they allowed themselves to be infected, especially by not taking the course of absolute neutrality toward the international wrangles of this world. He could not bless their being preoccupied more with their promised glorification in the heavenly kingdom than with the worldwide witness work that he had for them to do on earth in behalf of his newborn Messianic kingdom.[9]

The two pictures, martyrdom and vindication, and chastisement and restoration to favour, are not necessarily incompatible, although they might have seemed to sit more happily together had the earlier application of 'prophesying in sackcloth' (Revelation 11:3) to the Bible Students' mournful condition not been superseded by its application to the tone of their message. The point is minor and neither the divergence between the two pictures nor their possible harmonisation should be pressed too far, although the same author, Fred Franz, was responsible for both. In a different context, alternative views such as these might be regarded as legitimate variation within a single tradition or belief system. In the Watch Tower movement, however, the scope for legitimate variation is very limited, being restricted almost exclusively to those minor areas upon which the Society chooses not to legislate.

On either view, the end of the 1,260 days, the point at which Christ came to the heavenly temple and judgement upon all professing Christian began, led to the eventual revival of the Bible Students and the defeat of Babylon the Great. The release of the Society's directors in March 1919 marked both the restoration to life of the 'two witnesses' and the fall of Babylon.

The Faithful and Discreet Slave

A central tenet of Watch Tower ecclesiology is the belief that this movement is Jehovah's organisation, in contrast with all other religious and political institutions, which constitute Satan's organisation. This raises a question, however, which the Society has never directly addressed, namely, at what point did the movement become Jehovah's organisation? On the one hand, it could be maintained that the movement, having had its origins in the response to the divine initiative, has been Jehovah's organisation from the very beginning. On the other hand, it could be maintained that the movement, having first proved its faithfulness, was, at some comparatively late stage in its development, first adopted by Jehovah as his own.

The foregoing description of events between 1914 and 1919 is suggestive of the view that it was in 1919 that the Watch Tower movement first became Jehovah's organisation. A possible interpretation of the Society's teachings, as outlined so far, would be that all groups of professing Christians were, depending upon their Christian character and faithfulness, potential candidates for the divine commission in 1919. It happened to be the case that the Bible Students alone, despite their failings, were found to be acceptable. Whilst the literature may, at times, have seemed to imply this view, the Society has never explicitly stated it, despite the necessity, which has been recognised, to distance themselves from the prophetic interpretations of the early period. The continuity, however, between the Watch Tower movement under Russell's leadership and that into which it was later transformed by Rutherford, is clearly implied by the doctrine of the 'faithful and discreet slave'. Following his prophecy of his second presence, Jesus said,

> Who really is the faithful and discreet slave whom his master appointed
> over his domestics, to give them their food at the proper time? Happy
> is that slave if his master on arriving finds him doing so. Truly I say to
> you, He will appoint him over all his belongings. (Matthew 24:45-47)

This slave is identified collectively with all members of the 'little flock' currently living at any time in history from the beginning of Christianity until the time of the end. Since the number of the 'little flock' is limited to 144,000 (Revelation 7:4), the number of people comprising the composite 'slave' has almost always been very small indeed. The Watch Tower movement under Russell, then, constitutes a hitherto unprecedented flourishing of the 'slave' when, for the first time since the very earliest years of Christianity, it became possible to identify the 'slave' with a recognisable group. The master's returning and appointing his faithful slave over all his belongings, then, represents the same events as the revival of the 'two witnesses' and the commissioning of the modern day Ezekiel.[10]

The doctrine of the 'faithful and discreet slave' allows room for the view that the Watch Tower movement, as constituted under Russell's leadership, was already Jehovah's organisation, and that its commissioning for the prophetic role of the antitypical Ezekiel did not amount to its first becoming Jehovah's organisation. This, however, blurs the distinction which Russell had made between faithful Christians of the Protestant Reformation, for example, and his own movement. It appears that in the Society's current doctrine, Russell's movement occupies the middle ground between the time when individual faithful members of the 'little flock' received limited blessing and enlightenment, and the time when the divine initiative became the directive force.

This idea of a middle ground may offer a position in which consistency is possible, but it should not be assumed that this is the position to which the Society is committed. Nor, on the other hand, should any interpretation be pressed which leads to a clear inconsistency. The lack of clarity which remains, it should be noted, concerning the point at which the movement can be said to have become God's organisation, arises from the fact that as Russell's end-time calendar has been dismantled and all its components have been reinterpreted and brought forward into the twentieth century, so also has the movement's ecclesiology been brought forward. That is, the new ecclesiology, rather than being *extended* to embrace the whole of the movement's history, has been *transferred* so that it describes only the later period. The earlier period has been left with no theological description other than that which applies to faithful individuals from the first century onwards. This represents a further step in that long process of isolation which has been apparent from the beginning.

Daniel Reinterpreted

The foregoing description of the Bible Student's affairs between 1914 and 1919, whilst drawing largely upon an interpretation of passages from Revelation, implies some extensive revision in the interpretation of Daniel. The current understanding of the prophecies of Daniel was set out in 1958 in the book, *Your Will be Done on Earth*. It follows what is basically a traditional historicist approach with amendments which extend the fulfilment of the visions into the twentieth century. Again, chapters 11 and 12 are of main significance. The interpretation follows that of Russell until Daniel 11:27, when the reference moves from the third century AD to the late nineteenth century and the vision from that point is applied to the political struggles between the eastern and western powers from the time leading up to World War I until Armageddon. In this interpretation, first the German Reich and then Soviet Communism fulfil the role of the 'king of the north', whilst the 'king of the south' is identified with what the Society styles 'the Anglo-American dual world power'.[11]

Although this treatment of Daniel clearly derives from the historicist tradition, it abandons what had occupied a central place in that tradition, namely, the Papacy's demise at the end of 1,260 years of oppressing the saints. It allows the reapplication of the 1,260, 1,290, 1,335 and 2,300 days to periods in the twentieth century. The 1,260 days which, following the tradition, are identified with the similar period in Revelation 11:3, have already been dealt with. The event marking the end of that period, namely the almost complete suppression of the Bible Students' activities in 1918, constituted the removal of the 'continual sacrifice' which was one of two things identifying the beginning of the 1,290 days. The other was the setting up of the 'desolating abomination' (Daniel 12:11) which occurred when the Federal Council of the Churches of Christ in America gave its endorsement to the formation of the League of Nations. The Federal Council's executive committee, meeting in December 1918, adopted a Declaration which stated in part:

> The time has come to organize the world for truth and right, justice and humanity. To this end, as Christians we urge the establishment of a League of Free Nations at the coming Peace Conference [Paris, January 1919]. Such a League is not a mere political expedient; it is rather the political expression of the Kingdom of God on earth.[12]

The Paris Peace Conference, then, at which the Declaration was presented, marks the point at which Christendom, in defiance of the kingdom of God, declared her allegiance to a counterfeit and thereby set up the 'desolating abomination'. The 1,290 days, therefore, begin to count from the end of January 1919.[13]

The *terminus a quo* of the 1,290 days, though it receives a markedly different interpretation from any earlier treatment, nevertheless retains a link with the tradition in so far as it rests upon definitions of common terminology, namely, the removal of the 'continual sacrifice' and the 'desolating abomination'. The *terminus ad quem*, on the other hand, lacks even this tenuous link.

The 1,290 days must be treated from the standpoint of the lunar calendar. Hence, divine prophecy treats a month as being thirty days long. . . . Since 1,260 days in prophecy equal three years and six months, then 1,290 days equal three years and seven months. Counted from the close of January, 1919, where do those three years and seven months end? They bring us to the end of August and the beginning of September of 1922.[14]

The significant event of that month was an international convention of the Bible Students at Cedar Point, Ohio when Rutherford sought to stimulate renewed determination in the movement's preaching. The message to the Bible Students was summarised in what was to become a memorable slogan for them: 'Advertise, advertise, advertise, the King and his kingdom.' The message for the world at large was contained in a resolution adopted by the convention entitled 'A Challenge to World Rulers', which declared that:

The 'appointed times of the nations' had run out in 1914; that God's kingdom by Christ had then been set up in heaven; that the League of Nations was a fraud and must fail because God has decreed it thus.[15]

The end of the 1,290 days marked the beginning of the 1,335 days (Daniel 12:12) which, calculated on the same hybrid basis as the other periods, represent the three years, eight months and fifteen days from the end of the Cedar Point convention in September 1922 to May 1926. During the latter month there was a series of conventions, the final one of which was at London when, on 30 May, Rutherford delivered an address entitled 'Why World Powers Are Tottering – The Remedy', in which he identified the League of Nations as the 'desolating abomination' and called upon the British government to set a lead and withdraw its support.[16]

The London convention, in fulfilment of Daniel 12:12, then, marked the beginning of a 'period of happiness that has not ended and never will end'[17] for the faithful. But since the British government and governments throughout the world failed to respond to Rutherford's call to abandon the League of Nations, they thereby became guilty of the 'transgression of desolation' and the period of 2,300 days (Daniel 8:13, 14), the end of which would see the restoration of the sanctuary to its proper condition, began to count.[18]

The 2,300 days ended on 15 October 1932 when *The Watchtower* carried official notification of a significant reform in the way that elders in the local congregations of Jehovah's Witnesses were to be appointed. No longer was it considered proper for elders to be elected by democratic vote. Rather, though they continued to be nominated locally, the appointments were thenceforward confirmed centrally. By this reform, which is held to constitute the cleansing of the sanctuary, the Society was able to extend its control of the local congregations as elders became accountable to the Society and no longer to their congregations. This move eliminated the lingering opposition to Rutherford's leadership and paved the way for the creation of the uniformity of belief and policy which has apparently characterised the Witnesses for more than sixty years since.[19]

The Birth of the Kingdom

Having supplied some of the important dates in the new end-time calendar with the foregoing diversion through Daniel, Revelation's history of the last days can now be resumed. As has been noted earlier, the visions are not strictly sequential; chapter 12, rather than following on from where chapter 11 had ended, begins with the inauguration of the kingdom in 1914 and supplies additional detail to the picture that has already begun to be painted.

In this vision there is portrayed a woman who is about to give birth. A dragon having seven heads and ten horns is waiting to devour the child. However, once the child is born, he is caught away to heaven and the woman escapes to the wilderness (Revelation 12:1-6). The woman is identified with 'the Jerusalem above' (Galatians 4:26) which is

> Jehovah's universal organisation of spirit creatures that acts as his wife, both in serving him and in producing offspring. [20]

Support for this is found in the fact that the child, being caught away to God (Revelation 12:5), is thereby identified as a child of God and his mother, consequently, as the wife of God. She must be distinguished, however, from the 'New Jerusalem' which is the bride of Christ (Revelation 21:5). The birth of the child is

> the birth of God's Kingdom in 1914 as a reality, with Jesus – already in heaven for close to nineteen centuries – now enthroned as King. – Revelation 12:10.[21]

The first action of the newly enthroned king, who is here referred to as Michael, was to engage in battle with the dragon, who is identified with Satan, defeat him and expel him from heaven (Revelation 12:7-9). The enraged Satan has thereafter been confined to the earth and, beginning with the First World War, has caused havoc ever since.[22]

> Now when the dragon saw that it was hurled down to the earth, it persecuted the woman that gave birth to the male child. But the two wings of the great eagle were given to the woman, that she might fly into the wilderness; there is where she is fed for a time and times and half a time away from the face of the serpent. (Revelation 12:13,14)

At this point the vision resumes what had been introduced earlier, in verse 6. What is referred to is a period of three-and-a-half years of respite or protection from attack by Satan. Whereas the vision describes the woman herself as being attacked or protected, Watch Tower interpretation locates the fulfilment of the vision in a different realm.

> We may wonder how the dragon can persecute the woman, since she is in heaven and the dragon has now been cast down to the earth. Well, remember that the woman has children here on earth, her seed. Later in this vision, we are informed that Satan expresses his rage toward the woman by persecuting her seed. (Revelation 12:17) What happens to the woman's seed here on earth may be regarded as happening to the woman herself. (Compare Matthew 25:40) And the growing number of companions of the seed here on earth would also experience these persecutions.[23]

The 1,260 days when the woman was protected in the wilderness, then, are identified with the three-and-a-half years from the spring of 1919 to the autumn of 1922 when the Bible Students experienced a respite from adversity and were able to recuperate and reorganise.[24] Following this period of recuperation, Satan unleashed a further sustained attack upon the Witnesses.

> And the serpent disgorged water like a river from its mouth after the woman, to cause her to be drowned by the river. But the earth came to the woman's help, and the earth opened its mouth and swallowed up the river. (Revelation 12:15,16)

From 1922 onwards the Witnesses experienced considerable persecution. This reached its climax during the Second World War, particularly in Germany when thousands died in the Nazi concentration camps. In the United States of America they suffered discrimination and mob violence similar to their experience during the First World War.

However, 'the earth', namely elements within Satan's own organisation, came to the aid of the Witnesses. During the 1940s they won a series of favourable decisions in the United States Supreme Court which established their right to freedom of worship and religious practice. Finally, the Allied victory in 1945 brought an end to the persecution which they had suffered in Nazi Germany. Since then, although they have experienced persecution in various countries throughout the world, and the inevitability of it has continued to colour their understanding of their place in history, they have been allowed to flourish unmolested in most countries.[25]

The Coming Climax

The majority of the prophecies have had their fulfilments; what remains to be accomplished before Armageddon, however, is of major significance. Babylon the Great, the world empire of false religion, which came under divine judgement in 1918 and whose fall in 1919 was marked by the release from prison of the Watch Tower Society's directors, will, at last, be destroyed. This will come about not by the continuing decline in membership and loss of influence which have marked the years since her fall, but by devastation at the hands of her friends.

> The waters that you saw, where the harlot [Babylon the Great] is sitting, mean peoples and crowds and nations and tongues. And the ten horns that you saw, and the wild beast, these will hate the harlot and will make her devastated and naked, and will eat up her fleshy parts and will completely burn her with fire. (Revelation 17:15,16)

This will have its fulfilment when governments throughout the world turn upon all religious organisations, seeing them as a threat to their sovereignty.

> The nations will use the scarlet-colored wild beast, the United Nations, in destroying Babylon the Great. They do not act on their own initiative, for Jehovah puts it into their hearts 'even to carry out their one thought by giving their kingdom to the wild beast.' When the time comes, the nations will evidently see the need to strengthen the United Nations. They will give it teeth, as it were, lending it whatever authority and power they possess so that it can turn upon false religion and fight successfully against her 'until the words of God have been accomplished.' Thus, the ancient harlot will come to her complete end. And good riddance to her![26]

> What this will mean for the buildings of Babylon the Great and for her priests and other religious clergy and orders is something frightful to contemplate. We make no attempt to describe it.[27]

Although the Society forbear from supplying the details of Babylon's end, they leave no doubt about the way that the Witnesses might exercise their imaginations.

> What a thrilling moment it will be when, during the coming 'great tribulation' on this present system of things, the authentic news comes from all around the earth that the antitypical Jerusalem, Christendom, has fallen at the hands of Jehovah's executional forces! This will be a vindication of the modern-day Ezekiel class, to authenticate that they have not been a false prophet but have been a faithful watchman class in sounding out Jehovah's warnings to Christendom. The blood of clergymen and of other adherents of Christendom losing their lives at that time will be upon their own heads.[28]

Though it may seem at times that some of the Witnesses have an unhealthy preoccupation with the prospect of a gory end for their religious opponents, it should be realised that they do not expect that they themselves will escape entirely unscathed. Once Babylon has been destroyed, the Witnesses, who will be the only religious group remaining, will become the target and Satan, in the role of Gog of Magog (Ezekiel 38:14-16) will lead the nations in a final onslaught against them.

> They should not be surprised that they will have the whole world of mankind under Satan the Devil against them. Not amazed should they be even if military dictatorship world wide came. (*sic*)[29]

Their final adversity, however, will be shortened as Jehovah comes to their aid.

> The blood of Jehovah's Christian witnesses they are anxious to spill, but it will be their own blood that they will drink by the violent loss of their own lives. Panic – world panic outside the ranks of Jehovah's Christian witnesses! Gog's [Satan's] hordes will be thrown into confusion. Instead of keeping united to strike down Jehovah's worshipers as their victims, they will turn their swords against their own ranks. . . . Those whom this suicidal warfare among themselves does not kill off, Jehovah will execute.[30]

The last attack against the Witnesses, then, will culminate in Armageddon. The Millennium will have begun at last and the Witnesses will turn their attention to the massive task of clearing up the world-wide debris of the defeated system. Once that is completed, there will start a huge educational program for the benefit, especially, of the vast numbers of righteous people who will begin to be resurrected to the renewed paradise earth.

Table 5. *The New End Time Calendar*

4 October 1914
>End of the 'times of the Gentiles'.
>The Parousia and the 'Time of the end' begin.
>Christ enthroned in heaven.
>Beginning of the first 1,260 days – 'Two witnesses' prophesy in sackcloth.
>(Daniel 7:25; 12:7; Revelation 11:2)

27 March 1918
>End of the first 1,260 days.
>Coming of Christ to the temple.
>Dead in Christ resurrected.
>Judgement of all professing Christians begins.
>'Two witnesses' killed (Revelation 11:7).

January 1919
>Beginning of the 1,290 days (Daniel 12:11).
>League of Nations set up as 'abomination of desolation'.

March 1919
>Fall of 'Babylon the Great' (Revelation 18:2).
>Society's officers released from prison.
>'Two witnesses' restored to life.

Spring 1919
>Beginning of the second 1,260 days (Revelation 12:6,14).
>Respite and recuperation for the Bible Students.

September 1922
>End of the 1,290 days.
>Call to 'Advertise, advertise, advertise, the King and his Kingdom.'
>Beginning of the 1,335 days (Daniel 12:12).

Autumn 1922
>End of the second 1,260 days.
>Persecution of the Bible Students resumed.

May 1926
>End of the 1,335 days.
>British government called upon to withdraw support for the League of Nations.
>Failure to do so constituted the 'transgression of desolation'.
>Beginning of the 2,300 days (Daniel 8:14).

15 October 1932
>End of the 2,300 days.
>The Sanctuary restored to its rightful state by the ending of democratic elections
> of elders.

Not determined
>Destruction of Babylon the Great.
>Final attack by Gog of Magog against the Witnesses.
>Battle of Armageddon.
>Beginning of Christ's Thousand Years' Reign.

Notes

1. Listed below are the main sources for current doctrine. These are published anonymously, as is all of the Society's literature since the beginning of Nathan H. Knorr's presidency in 1942. *Your Will be Done on Earth* (1958), *The Nations Shall Know that I am Jehovah – How?* (1971), *God's Kingdom of a Thousand Years has Approached* (1973), *Man's Salvation out of World Distress at Hand* (1975),*Revelation – Its Grand Climax at Hand* (1988). The last-mentioned title largely supersedes the following two, to which, however, reference must still be made for material not carried forward into the more recent volume. *Babylon the Great has Fallen – God's Kingdom Rules* (1963), *Then is Finished the Mystery of God* (1969).

2. *Revelation – Its Grand Climax at Hand*, pp. 130f.

3. *Ibid.*, p. 131.

4. *Then is Finished the Mystery of God*, p. 288f.

5. *Your Will be Done on Earth*, p. 181.

6. *Then is Finished the Mystery of God*, pp. 263ff.

7. *Revelation – Its Grand Climax at Hand*, pp. 169f.

8. *The Nations Shall Know that I am Jehovah – How?*, pp. 61ff.

9. *Man's Salvation out of World Distress at Hand*, pp. 139f.

10. *God's Kingdom of a Thousand Years has Approached*, pp. 347ff.

11. *Your Will be Done on Earth*, pp. 264ff.

12. *Ibid.*, p. 206. (Quoting *Federal Council Bulletin*, Vol II, No.1, January 1919, pp. 12ff.)

13. *Ibid.*, p. 334.

14. *Ibid.*, p. 335.

15. *Ibid.*, p. 336.

16. *Ibid.*, pp. 213, 336ff.

17. *Ibid.*, p. 339.

18. *Ibid.*, pp. 210ff.

19. *Ibid.*, pp. 214ff.

20. *Revelation – Its Grand Climax at Hand*, p. 178.

21. *Ibid.*, p. 180.

22. *Ibid.*, pp. 181ff.

23. *Ibid.*, p. 183.

24. *Ibid.*, p. 184.

25. *Ibid.*, pp. 185f.

26. *Ibid.*, p. 258.

27. *Babylon the Great has Fallen*, p. 602.

28. *The Nations Shall Know that I am Jehovah*, p. 286.

29. *Ibid.*, p. 357.

30. *Ibid.*, p. 367.

Chapter Fifteen
The Security of 1914

It has already been noted that today's Watch Tower interpretation of the prophetic corpus does not rely to any great extent upon the kind of argument which had underpinned Russell's system. The argument from parallel dispensations has disappeared entirely and the majority of what had been generated within the historicist tradition by the application of the year-for-a-day principle has also disappeared. What is left of the original chronological approach is the same exposition of the 'seventy weeks' (Daniel 9:24-27) that Russell had espoused, with minor adjustment,[1] and a treatment of the 'times of the Gentiles' based upon a single line of argument where Russell had found two.

The result of this reduction in the importance of the chronological component is a system which can be all too easy to treat unsympathetically or to ridicule, much more so, indeed, than was Russell's. As long as one is prepared to study the chronological arguments which Russell put forward, it is possible to appreciate the rationale of his method and to understand the persuasiveness of his ideas. Turning to current Watch Tower doctrine, on the other hand, it seems that the whole system amounts to a set of dogmatic assertions concerning the fulfilment of the prophetic corpus, all of which derive support from each other but none of which has any external chronological supportive argument. 1914 alone is provided with such an external support, which must therefore underpin the whole system.

It should not be supposed, however, that the system's lack of direct external support renders it more vulnerable than was its predecessor. On the contrary, despite its apparent lack of a coherent underlying rationale, it may prove in the end to be a more durable system. 1914, upon which the whole structure is built, is well secured, not only by the chronology of the 'times of the Gentiles', but by certain important facts of history. The outbreak of war in 1914 heralded an era which, though by no means the only such era in history, does lend itself to description in the terms set out in Luke 21 and parallels. Belief in 1914 as the end of the 'times of the Gentiles', then, does not rest exclusively upon the arithmetic of Daniel 4. It rests also upon observed facts of history interpreted in the light of a particular view of Scripture. So even if what remains of the chronology which originally established 1914 as the crucial date were, though it is unlikely, to be dispensed with altogether, it should not be supposed that the significance of that year would thereby be undermined. The facts of history and the Witness view of Scripture remaining the same, it must be recognised that the Witnesses will continue for some considerable time to come to regard the end of the 'times of the Gentiles' as, quite simply, an observable fact.

The significance of the foregoing should not be underestimated, for it implies that two of the main processes whereby disillusionment may set in need not undermine the single most important element of the system. Whereas in recent years it has become increasingly common for some Witnesses to delve into the history of their prophetic beliefs,[2] the Society may have defused much of the impact of this sort of probing by a policy of being a little more open about past beliefs than was once the case. *God's Kingdom of a Thousand Years has Approached*, in particular, though it distorts the original doctrines and misrepresents the significance of some of the amendments which began to be brought in during the latter part of Rutherford's presidency, has seriously weakened the position of those who would seek to discredit the Society simply by listing failed predictions.

It is illuminating at this point to compare the perceived validation of today's beliefs with that of the original system. Whereas Russell's system had received partial confirmation by the apparent validation of its methods (particularly the year-for-a-day principle) but still awaited its major confirmation in the fulfilment of expectations, the current system has already received much of its major confirmation to the satisfaction of its adherents. Further, those components of Russell's system which had been most strikingly confirmed, namely the prophecies of the 'seventy weeks' and the 1,260 days, belonged to the wider millennialist tradition. In Witness doctrine, on the other hand, the interpretation of the events of 1914, which provides the clearest validation of the system, is the peculiar property of the Watch Tower movement. Consequently, what is now seen to validate the millennialist beliefs is seen to validate not any wider shared tradition, but only the movement itself.

Although the application of the 'seventy weeks' to the period culminating in Jesus' ministry retains its persuasiveness, the passage of time and the recovery of the Roman Catholic Church from its humiliation at the end of the eighteenth century have robbed the traditional interpretation of the 1,260 days of much of its persuasiveness. The significance of 1914, on the other hand, seems likely to remain undiminished. So if the perceived beginning of the 'time of the end' need not be undermined by the exposure to scrutiny of elements of that system in which its place was first established, nor will it necessarily be undermined by the continued delay of expectations still awaited. The 'observable' nature of the end of the 'times of the Gentiles' is likely to remain intact for many years to come and to provide good reason for perseverance, just as the apparent successes of nineteenth-century premillennialism kept the tradition alive in the face of major disillusionment.

External Support

There is an important additional line of external support for Watch Tower millennialism, which may be summarised as an argument from the uniqueness of the movement. Of particular significance in this regard is the understanding of one of the signs of the approaching end:

This good news of the kingdom will be preached in all the inhabited earth for a witness to all the nations; and then the end will come.(Matthew 24:14)

This prophecy is applied, naturally, to the Watch Tower movement's preaching but it is interesting to note that it is used in two different ways. First, the fact that the kingdom is being preached as never before is offered as further evidence that Jesus' prophecy of the end is in the course of fulfilment.[3] Second, however, given that it is accepted that the world has now reached its 'last days', the distinctive nature of the Witnesses' preaching is offered as confirmation that they are the one religious organisation through which God is operating.[4]

Though it should be clear that the argument which is generated by putting these two ideas together is circular, amounting to the contention that the fact that the Witnesses' preach their message is confirmation of the truth of that message, it should be appreciated that the argument from distinctiveness is a wide-ranging one in which it is more important to give due weight to the contributory elements than to expose its circularity. Indeed, the argument is never deployed by the Society in its most obviously circular form.

The fall of Babylon and the Watch Tower movement's release from bondage involved far more than simply the release from prison of Rutherford and his fellow directors in 1919. In fact, it involved the whole movement's rejection of everything that is sinful or of pagan origin in Christendom:

Get out of her, my people, if you do not want to share with her in her sins, and if you do not want to receive part of her plagues. (Revelation 18:4)

This rejection of Babylon's sinfulness involves, especially, three areas: the doctrinal, the political and the moral. Of primary importance in doctrinal matters are the Society's rejection of the Trinity and the related doctrine of the divine name. The Trinity is held to have originated in ancient Babylon and to have been incorporated into Christendom's teachings in order to make them more palatable for pagans for whom it was expedient to convert to Christianity.[5] The non-trinitarian doctrine of Jesus Christ holds that he is the one referred to in the prologue to John's Gospel as the Word, but that he is a separate and distinct being from God – he is a god, but not The God.[6]

Also of special importance amongst the distinctive doctrines of the Watch Tower is their teaching concerning the divine name, 'Jehovah'.

God for the first time turned his attention to the nations to take out of them a people for his name. (Acts 15:14)

Though Russell had made a habit of using the name 'Jehovah', it was from 1931 in particular, with the adoption of the name 'Jehovah's Witnesses' that it began to take on the central significance which it now has. The contention is that when Jesus said, 'I have made your name manifest to the men you gave me out of the world' (John 17:6), that he meant, quite literally, that he had departed from the superstitious custom of the age and had taught his disciples to use the name instead of making the usual substitutions. For that reason, the *New World Translation of the Holy Scriptures* has the name 'Jehovah' wherever the New Testament quotes from an Old Testament source in which the Tetragrammaton, the four Hebrew consonants representing the divine name, appears. All Witnesses learn to use the name just as easily as anyone else uses the name 'Jesus'.

Their distinctiveness is shown also in their refusal to be involved in politics.

'They are no part of the world, just as I am no part of the world' (John 17:16). For this reason Jehovah's Witnesses take no part in any political activity, even to the point of not exercising their democratic right to vote. Their political neutrality is shown especially in their refusal to be conscripted for military service.

Traditional morality has a high priority amongst the Witnesses. Any infringement of the moral code will, unless it is an isolated incident and proper repentance is evident, lead to expulsion from the congregation. In this regard they are always ready to emphasise their distinctiveness. All major denominations, the Society frequently asserts, have adopted a moral laxity which falls far short of Christian standards.[7]

All of the foregoing points, but certainly the doctrinal matters, deserve far more extensive treatment than is possible here. In the present context the point to be emphasised is that these areas of belief and practice provide for the Witnesses a real sense of their own religious uniqueness. It all amounts to evidence that, as was implied in the prophecies, the faithful have been coming out of Babylon, the world empire of false religion, during the 'time of the end'. So, the isolation from the Christian mainstream, which has progressed since the early days, is seen as confirmation of the correctness of their position. All the perceived failures of the mainstream, whether doctrinal, political or moral, as well as declining numbers and influence, also lend support to this view.

What this amounts to is that, where Russell's system had been underpinned by a body of chronological argument which gained credibility from its coherence, today's Watch Tower system is underpinned by the interpretation of actual states of affairs which can, to the satisfaction of the Witnesses, properly be described as observable facts. Thus, it is 'observable fact' that the 'times of the Gentiles' ended in 1914, that the doctrines of the Watch Tower movement show beyond all doubt that only they have responded to the call to come out of Babylon, and that Babylon has been judged and is suffering the consequences of its godlessness. All of this must provide good reason to suppose that the Watch Tower movement may have the potential to survive largely unchanged into the twenty-first century.

The Achilles' Heel

Despite the considerable potential strength noted above, however, the Watch Tower movement has some serious weaknesses which could, depending upon how they are handled by the leadership, undermine its stability in the future. First, there must be some doubt concerning the ability of the Society's leaders to acknowledge the relationship of their current doctrine of the Millennium to its precursors, not only within the millennialist tradition but also within their own movement. It was a similar lack of appreciation of basic principles which contributed to the unsatisfactory nature of the amendments put forward in *The Finished Mystery* and which, perhaps, contributed to the *ad hoc* nature of the process of reconstruction begun by Rutherford. This raises the question whether any future amendments which may be found to be necessary will satisfactorily deal with existing problems without raising new ones.

Evidence of the Society's failure to understand or, more seriously, misrepresentation of thin[8] the history of its own doctrines is found in the book *God's Kingdom of a Thousand Years has Approached*. It is there pointed out that the revision of Old Testament chronology which was published in 1943 in the book *The Truth Shall Make You Free* included the recognition that the period of the Judges of ancient Israel, and hence, also, the Jewish age itself, was one century shorter than had previously been believed. This, it was suggested, would affect the date when the Christ's Second Presence became due.[9]

The revision did, of course, completely remove the possibility of any new argument from parallel dispensations, but the date of the Second Presence did not rest solely upon that in Russell's system. *God's Kingdom*, however, makes no mention of this argument which had, in fact, disappeared from the system long before 1943. Instead, it offers what is either a misunderstanding or a misrepresentation of the significance of the revision:

This moved forward the end of six thousand years of man's existence into the decade of the 1970's. Naturally this did away with the year 1874 C.E. as the date of the return of the Lord Jesus Christ and the beginning of his invisible presence.[10]

Whilst it is true that Russell did observe that, on his understanding of Old Testament chronology, six millennia from the creation extended to 1872, he did not determine the beginning of the Second Presence on that basis. True, he understood it to mark the beginning of the Millennial age which, it will be remembered, was regarded as beginning in stages.[11] But the Second Presence had a precise beginning, 1874, which was fixed by the argument from the Jubilees and the year-for-a-day interpretation of the 1,335 days of Daniel 12:12 as well as the parallel dispensations. Only the latter was affected by the revised Old Testament chronology; and, given that it was discarded altogether and not revised, the date of the Second Presence should continue to be supported by its other derivations and to remain unaffected by the new chronology. The idea that the millennial kingdom was to be concurrent with the seventh millennium of human existence was, in Russell's system, an inference from the timing of the Second Presence as established by the prophetic material. The inexact correspondence between the two dates was explained on the supposition that two years must have elapsed between the creation of Adam and the Fall. The Millennium, then, would begin after six thousand years of human sinfulness.[12] But if that is the case, then it must be supposed that if any revision of the six thousand years affects the timing of the Second Presence, then the latter must be assigned to a date following the revised end of those six millennia.

The writer of *God's Kingdom*, then, though he has recognised that the revision of Old Testament chronology had implications for Russell's system, has failed to show that he understands precisely what those implications were. He has failed also to acknowledge that the timing of the Second Presence had already been reassigned to 1914 at least six years before the publication of the amended Old Testament chronology.[13] The 1943 amendment, then, despite *God's Kingdom*, contributed nothing at that time to the revision of the end-time calendar. It did, however, provide the basis for much later speculation concerning the year 1975, which was to prove a major embarrassment.

The potential vulnerability of the Watch Tower movement arises not only from the fact that the updating of its doctrines may now be in the hands of people who do not fully understand the history of those doctrines, but also from the fact that the history appears, at times, to be deliberately misrepresented. So although the publication of *God's Kingdom* may have reduced the impact of the simple lists of failed predictions which are found in much of the literature of their religious opponents, deeper probing still reveals much about which the Society has not yet been open.

Of particular importance in this regard is the failure of 1925 and the Society's response to it. That was the year which, as Rutherford had clearly indicated in *Millions Now Living Will Never Die*, was to see the resurrection of the 'ancient worthies' and the glorification of the last remaining members of the 'little flock'.[14] When those events did not occur, large numbers of Bible Students left the movement. Unlike 1914, however, which saw events that were to prove capable of incorporation into an amended interpretation of the prophecies, 1925 provided no obvious material for such revision. Rutherford persevered without being able to give any adequate explanation of the failure, until the date was dropped altogether and the relatively small number of those who remained loyal to the Society were eventually outnumbered by newcomers who were largely unaware of the failure.

God's Kingdom, despite its apparent frankness concerning past failure, makes no mention of 1925. For a long time, whenever the Society referred to the difficulties of that year, they placed the blame upon those who seceded.

> The year 1925 started very promisingly. . . . However, some had their own personal convictions with respect to the year 1925. Would they let themselves be admonished by *The Watchtower* of January 1, 1925? It cautioned: 'The year 1925 is here. With great expectation Christians have looked forward to this year. Many have confidently expected that all members of the body of Christ will be changed to heavenly glory during the year. This may be accomplished. It may not be. In his own due time God will accomplish his purposes concerning his own people.'[15]

The fact that Bible Students left in such large numbers may have predisposed the minority who remained with Rutherford to acquiesce in placing the blame for the embarrassment upon the seceders. It used to be the case that Witnesses who were aware of the difficulties of that year usually supposed that the problem arose because some individuals were too ready to develop their own ideas instead of following the lead of the Society. Since the publication in 1993 of *Jehovah's Witnesses, Proclaimers of God's Kingdom*, there is more awareness of the problems of those years. Still, however, the blame is placed upon the defectors.

> No doubt disappointment over the date was a factor, but in some instances the roots went deeper. Some individuals argued against the need to participate in the house-to-house ministry. Certain ones . . . became aggressive in opposing the organisation.[16]

This tendency of the Society's leaders to place the blame for disillusionment upon those who were disillusioned rather than those who fostered the expectations which subsequently failed, seems to have set a pattern for dealing with similar situations. During the mid 1960s the literature began to direct attention to the year 1975 as the end of the sixth millennium since the creation of humanity. Although it is true that it was never stated unequivocally that Armageddon and the beginning of the millennial kingdom would occur in that year, it was clearly and repeatedly implied.

How appropriate it would be for Jehovah God to make of this coming seventh period of a thousand years a sabbath period of rest and release, a great Jubilee sabbath for the proclaiming of liberty throughout the earth to all its inhabitants! . . . Prophetically Jesus Christ, when on earth nineteen centuries ago, said concerning himself: 'For Lord of the sabbath is what the Son of man is.' (Matthew 12:8) It would not be by mere chance or accident but would be according to the loving purpose of Jehovah God for the reign of Jesus Christ, the 'Lord of the sabbath,' to run parallel with the seventh millennium of man's existence.[17]

As late as the spring of 1975, Frederick Franz, then Vice-President of the Society and later to become President, stated at an assembly of Jehovah's Witnesses in Ontario, Canada, that the Society's leaders were looking forward with confidence to what would transpire in the autumn of that year.[18]

The summer of 1975 saw the publication of *Man's Salvation out of World Distress at Hand*, a title which, coming at the end of several years intense speculation, might have seemed to herald the great climax at last. However, it appears to have been as much concerned with the need to deal with possible disillusionment as with the nearness of Armageddon. This was the book in which was found the Society's strongest criticism of the early Bible Students for their eager anticipation of the fulfilment of their expectations.

They needed to readjust their thinking and their way to the new and unexpected situation that now opened up before them. They had been 'consecrated' to their God, not to a certain date such as 1914 or 1918 C.E., but for eternity.[19]

The delinquent remnant of spiritual Israelites could repent of their faulty course, when once it came to their attention.[20]

The lesson for disappointed Witnesses seems clear enough: they must not allow themselves to expect too much. Indeed Franz, speaking again in Ontario one year after his earlier expression of confidence, said:

Do you know why nothing happened in 1975? It was because you expected something to happen.[21]

What is not so clear, however, is how they might have heeded this lesson in advance, for it has long been obligatory upon the Witnesses to accept the Society's teachings without demur.

Statistics may conceal the real impact of the failure of 1975 and any consequent dissatisfaction with the Society's leadership. So far as numbers are concerned, the result amounted to little more than a temporary setback in the movement's steady expansion. However, what the statistics do not reveal is a turnover of membership which, though difficult to quantify, seems to constitute a greater problem for the Society now than in earlier years. It has always been the case that the Witnesses have experienced a high rate of loss, as significant numbers of new members have lapsed after a brief time with the movement. What seems to have begun to happen in recent years, however, has been that this turnover in membership has included Witnesses of long standing, and in some places substantial numbers have left and have formed independent groups.[22]

This drift from the Society does not threaten to become as serious as were the defections during Rutherford's presidency, but they are symptomatic of a movement which is facing difficulties in handling the doubts of many of its members. The situation has not been helped by the defection of some leading Witnesses including Raymond Franz, a member of the Governing Body, and Edward Dunlap, a former registrar of the Society's missionary college.

Though the dissatisfaction felt within the movement following the failure of 1975 may by now have subsided, the recent substantial losses have swelled the ranks of the Society's opponents and have created a far better-informed opposition than hitherto. Whether or not this may increase the movement's vulnerability will depend to a large extent upon whether any further crises occur and, if so, how they are handled.

Notes

1. *This Means Everlasting Life*, pp. 81ff. The only adjustment which has been made is in recognition of the fact that there is no year 0 between dates BC and AD. This has been accommodated by retarding dates BC by one year with the result that the dates in the fulfilment of the prophecies remain intact.
2. M. J. Penton, *Apocalypse Delayed*, p. 8.
3. *Things in Which it is Impossible for God to Lie*, p. 327.
4. *The Truth that Leads to Eternal Life*, p. 129.
5. *Babylon the Great has Fallen*, pp. 475ff.
6. *The Word – Who is He According to John?*, pp. 3ff.
7. *The Truth that Leads to Eternal Life*, pp. 125f.
8. Raymond Franz has pointed out to me in private correspondence that all of the Society's books published between 1942 and 1976 were, with a few exceptions written by the same man, Fred Franz. This strongly suggests that where more recent writings appear to betray a lack of understanding of earlier doctrinal statements, it is perhaps more likely to be deliberate misrepresentation.
9. *God's Kingdom of a Thousand Years has Approached*, p. 209.
10. *Ibid.*, pp. 209ff.
11. C. T. Russell, *The Time is at Hand*, pp. 51, 242.
12. C. T. Russell, *Thy Kingdom Come*, p. 127.
13. J. F. Rutherford, *Enemies*, p. 315.
14. Above, Chapter 12.
15. *1987 Yearbook of Jehovah's Witnesses*, pp. 131f.
16. *Jehovah's Witnesses, Proclaimers of God's Kingdom*, p. 633.
17. *Life Everlasting – In Freedom of the Sons of God*, p. 30.
18. Penton, *op. cit.*, pp. 99f.
19. *Man's Salvation out of World Distress at Hand*, p. 114.
20. *Ibid.*, p. 140.
21. Penton, *op. cit.*, p. 100.
22. *Ibid.*, pp. 122f.

Chapter Sixteen

The Response to Crisis

Over the past few years the question why the climax which Jehovah's Witnesses have long expected has not yet occurred has become more and more insistent. The Society's leaders have, therefore, been under growing pressure to provide satisfactory answers. The movement's long term future, then, will depend to some extent upon the capacity of the current system of beliefs to provide adequate descriptions of developing world affairs, and also upon the adequacy of the amendments to that system which are now beginning to be put forward to accommodate the protracted delay of Armageddon.

The situation which the Witnesses may face in the coming years, however, may not amount to anything on quite the same scale as those crises of the past which threatened the movement's existence. Nevertheless, much of the strength with which the early Bible Students overcame the worst of their crises may no longer be available to the Witnesses today, for the most creative responses to crisis belong to that phase of the movement's history from which today's Society has distanced itself.

The early Watch Tower movement, having had its origin within the disarray following the failure of William Miller's predictions, shared with its contemporary Seventh-day Adventism the experience of disillusionment at the very outset. Where Adventism, however, effectively reduced the scope for future disillusionment, Russell was bolder and led his followers through a series of minor crises as he attempted to identify the time for the glorification of the 'little flock'. By the time 1914 was reached, the Bible Students already had some considerable experience of dealing with possible disillusionment. This may well have helped them through the difficult period immediately following 1914, until it became apparent how events might be incorporated into the system. By the time that recovery from the disappointment of 1914 had begun, the experience of the Bible Students had been that their crises had resulted in the steady clarification of their doctrine. Indeed, the disappointment of 1914 gave way in due course to the perception of events of that year as a resounding confirmation of what had been expected or, at least, of what ought to have been expected. An element of this perception remains in Watch Tower understanding of their own history, but its capacity to supply strength in the face of further crisis has, it seems to me, been much eroded.

The diminishing ability of the Witnesses to draw strength from the experience of the early Bible Students arises from more than the mere passage of time. The secessions during Rutherford's presidency allowed the Society to place the blame for disillusionment upon Bible Students who, it is claimed, expected too much, rather than with Rutherford who fostered those expectations. The result is a tendency amongst the Witnesses to associate past disillusionment with inadequate discipleship, a view which is seen to be confirmed in the belief that the most seriously disillusioned, in leaving the movement, thereby left Jehovah's organisation. A further effect of this shifting of the blame has been the reduced need for the Society's response to crisis to include clarification of doctrine. Thus, whereas the early crises generated amendments to the doctrine, some of which are substantial, neither 1925 nor 1975 brought any comparable result. The time may be coming, however, when a return to a more creative response to potential disillusionment will be called for.

Revision for the Future

There are two areas in particular to which attention must be addressed. First, developing world affairs may call for accommodation, especially as the continued identification of Soviet Communism with the 'king of the north' (Daniel 11:40-43) begins to lose its plausibility. The view in 1958 had been that Soviet Communism and Anglo-America would continue in hostile coexistence until Armageddon.

> In the confused fighting between the 'two kings' as crazed enemies of Jehovah God and his kingdom, the 'kings' will have opportunity and occasion to try out and use their frightful, deadly weapons of all kinds against each other.[1]

Immediately before Armageddon, the final onslaught by Gog of Magog against the Witnesses was expected to come when

> the king of the north sets out to destroy the 'beauteous land,' to wipe it off the face of the earth. In this course he acts as an earthly instrument of Gog of Magog, who is Satan the Devil. Ezekiel 38:14-17; 39:1-6 foretells that Gog with his earthly hordes actually invades the 'beauteous land' of restored spiritual Israel. This becomes the time for Jehovah to begin the war of his great day.[2]

Some amendment to the 1958 view has already occurred. By 1971 the final attack against the Witnesses was expected to involve no single political system, but all of the world's governments.[3] Whether any further amendment may be forthcoming in order to take account of the breaking up of the Soviet Union remains to be seen. That may not, however, be felt to be necessary, especially in view of the fact that another of the expected events preceding Armageddon is the apparent establishment of peace throughout the world.

> When will Armageddon come? The Bible does not say. But world events in fulfillment of prophecy indicate that it will be very soon. The Bible clearly foretells an event that will be an immediate precursor. The apostle Paul says: 'Whenever it is that they are saying, "Peace and Security!" then sudden destruction is to be instantly upon them.' (1 Thessalonians 5:3)[4]

This does, perhaps, suggest a way forward in which the end of the 'Cold War' and the early demise of the Communist 'king of the north' might be incorporated into the system as it stands at present, without too much revision. Indeed, simply allowing the precise details of the 1958 interpretation of Daniel 11 to disappear from view may be all that is required.

A second area where the need for revision has already been recognised may yet prove to be troublesome. This concerns the understanding of Matthew 24:34 which, it was long believed, identifies the generation which will see the coming of Armageddon. This verse, coming towards the end of Jesus' prophecy regarding the signs of his Second Presence, was understood by the Society to refer not mainly or exclusively to the generation of Jesus' day but, more importantly, to that which saw the first indications of the prophecy's fulfilment in 1914.

> Persons born even as much as fifty years ago could not see '*all* these things.' They came on the scene after the foretold events were already under way. But there are people still living who were alive in 1914 and saw what was happening then and who were old enough that they still remember those events. This generation is getting up in years now. A great number of them have already passed away in death. Yet Jesus very pointedly said: 'This generation will *by no means* pass away until all these things occur.' [Matt 24:34] Some of them will still be alive to see the end of this wicked system. This means that only a short time is left before the end comes![5]

This verse, more than any other, has kept alive a real sense of urgency amongst Jehovah's Witnesses, especially as the onset of Armageddon has become more and more distant from the events to which the chronological arguments apply. Indeed, every issue of the magazine *Awake!* has for many years carried the words:

> This magazine builds confidence in the Creator's promise of a peaceful and secure new world before the generation that saw the events of 1914 passes away.

The Watchtower of 1 November 1995, however, took the very bold step of reinterpreting this crucial verse. No longer is it held to identify any particular generation which might be associated with any period of time. The new application is much more flexible.

> Eager to see the end of this evil system, Jehovah's people have at times speculated about the time when the 'great tribulation' would break out, even tying this to calculations of what is the lifetime of a generation since 1914. However, we 'bring a heart of wisdom in,' not by speculating about how many years or days make up a generation, but by thinking about how we 'count our days' in bringing joyful praise to Jehovah.[6]

> [Jesus] stated concerning himself: 'the Son of man ... must undergo many sufferings and be *rejected by this generation*. Moreover, *just as it occurred in the days of Noah*, so it will be also in the days of the Son of man.' (Luke 17:24-26) Thus, Matthew chapter 24 and Luke chapter 17 make the same comparison. In Noah's day 'all flesh that had ruined its way on the earth' and that was destroyed at the Flood was '*this generation*.' In Jesus' day the apostate Jewish people that were rejecting Jesus was '*this generation*' – Genesis 6:11, 12; 7:1.

> Therefore, in the final fulfillment of Jesus' prophecy today, 'this generation' apparently refers to the peoples of the earth who see the sign of Christ's presence but fail to mend their ways. In contrast, we as Jesus' disciples refuse to be molded by the life-style of 'this generation.'[7] (Emphasis original)

The reference of the expression 'this generation', then, constantly moves on. It is all people during the 'time of the end', however long that might turn out to be, who fail to heed the Witnesses' message. Although the *Watchtower* article which spells out this interesting change of interpretation insists that the revision does not imply that Armageddon is further off than hitherto believed, the change does mean that the 'time of the end' can now be indefinitely extended.

With the simple redefinition of a single expression, the Society has probably gone a long way towards securing its long-term future, though how many Witnesses will now leave in disillusionment before some measure of stability is restored remains to be seen. But the system has now been rescued from further dependence upon developing world affairs for its confirmation and those Witnesses who are willing to continue to accept the Society's leadership can simply get on with the task in hand as they await Armageddon for as long as may be necessary. In effect, the Society has reached the same point in its development that Seventh-day Adventism reached in the late nineteenth century, when a redefinition of the cleansing of the sanctuary allowed the retention of William Miller's system without the need for further revision.

If the Society is to take full advantage of the respite which they may have gained by this bold revision, then it will be necessary for them to concentrate upon other distinctive areas of doctrine in order to displace the Witnesses' active concern with the coming climax. Such a displacement might allow the passage of time to reduce their commitment to belief in a limited though indeterminate period within which the climax must come.

Indeed, during the latest period of the movement's development there has been a degree of displacement of the chronological approach to the prophetic corpus. Emphasis has been placed instead upon the ways in which events since 1914 have fulfilled the prophecies. Together with this there has been increasing emphasis upon the movement's distinctiveness which has given increased importance to other doctrines and practices. This has been only a partial displacement, however, since the movement's distinctiveness has become an essential element of their millennialist doctrine. Without the doctrine of the kingdom, the Society's anti-trinitarian teaching and its doctrine of the divine name would appear to have only reduced appeal, whilst its insistence that the medical practice of blood transfusion is wrong would become even harder to accept. That being so, there must be little scope for further displacement involving these areas.

The most likely area in which further limited displacement might take place is its ethical teaching, which has already, over the past several years, been given an increasingly prominent place. Whereas it is unlikely that Watch Tower ethics will eclipse expectations of the coming kingdom, it is a vitally important element in the Society's doctrine and one which, unlike so many other important elements, carries no hint of either heresy or eccentricity. It is, rather, a strict version of an ethical stance which is shared by many in the Christian mainstream and which, apparently, is perceived by large numbers to be suffering steady erosion. At a time when the bold reinterpretation of 'this generation' might prove disillusioning to many Witnesses and so threaten to weaken the Watch Tower movement, any perceived lowering of moral standards within the mainstream is likely to be seen by the Witnesses as confirmation of their own distinctiveness and could compensate for increasingly evident internal weaknesses.

Towards the Twenty-first Century

Though it seems unlikely that the Watch Tower movement will experience defections on the same scale as during Rutherford's presidency, it seems equally unlikely that it will regain the stability which was enjoyed for many years following the Second World War. Loss of members has always been a feature of the movement but until now has usually been outnumbered by steady increases. Losses, however, will almost certainly continue and most probably accelerate. This will contribute to an increasingly well-informed opposition. Hitherto, Witnesses have been shielded to a great extent from the pressure which dissidents could exert, by the strict policy of ostracising all who are disfellowshipped or who formally withdraw their membership. Whereas this policy has contributed towards the movement's imperviousness to informed criticism and, hence, to its stability, it seems to me that the time is coming when it will no longer be possible for the Society to exert such control over its members. As the informed opposition becomes increasingly visible, greater pressure will be required to ensure that their criticisms remain unheard by faithful Witnesses. Whether Jehovah's Witnesses will continue unquestioningly to accept the Society's authority, however, remains to be seen. Indeed, it is possible that stability will only be achieved in the coming years by abandoning the rigid requirement for doctrinal conformity amongst all Witnesses. To allow some limited scope for variation of opinion would diminish the impact of critics outside the movement.

The idea of permissible variation in doctrinal matters, however, would be a very difficult concept for many in the movement to handle, for it would seem to amount to allowing criticism from within of the 'faithful and discreet slave', an offence which has hitherto attracted the harshest discipline. For that reason, such relaxation may be regarded as a policy of last resort.

The Influence of the Watch Tower Society

The rigid separateness which the Witnesses maintain from all formal and informal institutions of the wider community has, perhaps, diminished the influence which they have been able to exert. Whereas their membership in some countries may be comparable with some of the smaller mainstream denominations, they have had little corresponding impact upon political, commercial, social or religious affairs. Their influence has been confined almost exclusively to their own members and that large but indeterminate number of people who have associated with them for a time but who have made no lasting commitment.

Any substantial increase in the Witnesses' rate of turnover of membership, however, is likely to swell the small number of disaffected Witnesses who become attached to mainstream denominations. Such people, it should be recognised, though they have rejected the leadership of the Watch Tower Society, often maintain many of the beliefs and attitudes which are characteristic of that movement. And they frequently display a willingness to be involved in evangelism and Bible study. Those most eager to pursue a calling to active discipleship are likely to gravitate towards those churches which are most willing to accommodate local lay leadership.

What this amounts to is that any loss of credibility amongst Jehovah's Witnesses of Watch Tower millennialism, which might seriously undermine the movement's stability, will increase the numbers of people, schooled in Watch Tower theology, seeking to exercise a ministry elsewhere. If the steady increase in membership which the Witnesses have maintained for the past sixty years were to be reversed, it would not represent merely the decline of a movement which has seemed, to the mainstream, to be at best an irrelevance and at worst a nuisance. Rather, it would represent the dispersal into the mainstream of an influence which has until now appeared too remote to cause concern.

Notes

1. *Your Will be Done on Earth*, p. 297.
2. *Ibid.*, pp. 298f.
3. *The Nations Shall Know that I Am Jehovah – How?*, pp. 362ff.
4. *The Watchtower*, 1 April 1990, p. 9.
5. *The Truth that Leads to Eternal Life*, p. 95.
6. *The Watchtower*, 1 November 1995, p. 17
7. *Ibid.*, p. 19.

Appendix One
Glossary of Millennialist Terms

Antitype:
See Type and Antitype below.

Armageddon:
The final conflict when Satan, together with his entire organisation, both physical and spiritual, is to be defeated (see Revelation 16:16).

Dispensationalism:
A theory developed by John Nelson Darby (1800-1882), in which history is divided into epochs, or dispensations, according to the way in which God is dealing with mankind. The dispensations usually identified are: the Edenic, the ante-diluvian, the post-diluvian, the patriarchal, the Jewish, the Gospel, and the future ages.

Futurism:
The belief that much of the prophetic corpus is to have its fulfilment, not in the course of world history, but only at the 'time of the end', and that prophecy is silent about events between Jesus' first coming and his return.

Historicism:
The belief that prophecies in Scripture, particularly those of Daniel and Revelation, chart the course of world history from the time of the Babylonian exile until the 'time of the end'.

Last days:
In modern Watch Tower doctrine, an alternative designation for the 'time of the end'. In Russell's system the 'last days' referred to he final period of the 'time of the end'.

Millennium:
A period of one thousand years following Armageddon, during which Christ rules as king from heaven and earth is restored to a paradise. At the end of the Millennium, Satan is to be allowed a brief period of freedom before his final complete destruction (see Revelation 20:1-10).

Parallel dispensations:

Charles Taze Russell's belief that the Jewish and Gospel ages are of equal duration, and that the timing of certain events at the close of the Jewish age is a prophetic indication of the timing of certain corresponding events at the close of the Gospel age.

Parousia:

The Greek word often rendered 'coming' in references to the return of Christ. Watch Tower doctrine emphasises that aspect of its meaning which implies Christ's continuing presence throughout the 'time of the end' and, therefore, always translates it as 'presence'.

Postmillennialism:

The belief that Jesus' second coming, or Parousia, follows the Millennium, which would begin following a period of gradual improvement in human society during which the Church's mission is to bring the world to Christ.

Premillennialism:

The belief that the Parousia precedes the inauguration of the Millennium.

Seventy weeks:

A period of 490 (70 x 7) years which are to elapse between the decree for the rebuilding of Jerusalem until the appearance of Messiah. The Watch Tower Society, closely following the historicist tradition, applies this to the period ending in AD 29 with the baptism of Jesus. Futurist interpreters apply only sixty-nine weeks to the period culminating in Jesus' ministry and hold that the seventieth week is still in the future (see Daniel 9:24-27).

Time:

A year, especially in prophecy (see Daniel 12:7; Revelation 12:14) which, in the millennialist tradition, is understood to be 360 days.

Time of the end:

In current Watch Tower doctrine this is the period following the end of the 'times of the Gentiles' and before Armageddon. In Russell's system, it referred to the period following 1799 (the end of the 1,260 days of Daniel 12:6, 7 and Revelation 11:3) and before the end of the 'times of the Gentiles'.

Times of the Gentiles:

The period during which theocracy is in abeyance, from the end of the ancient Jewish monarchy, marked by the beginning of the Babylonian exile, 607 BC, until the inauguration of the kingdom of God in heaven in AD 1914 (see Luke 21:24).

Type and Antitype:

A type is an event, person or institution which points forward prophetically to some corresponding reality, particularly, in Watch Tower doctrine, during the 'time of the end'. For example, the ancient Jewish monarchy is a type of the kingdom of God. An antitype is that which is thus foreshadowed.

Appendix Two
Dramatis Personae

A summary of the main apocalyptic symbols as interpreted in current Watch Tower doctrine.

Ezekiel 38 – Gog of Magog:
Satan the Devil, especially in his role leading the final onslaught against the Witnesses (*The Nations Shall Know That I Am Jehovah*, p. 354).

Daniel 2 – Nebuchadnezzar's dream image:
Golden head: The Babylonian Empire beginning with Nebuchadnezzar (*Your Will Be Done on Earth*, p. 114).
Silver breast and arms: The Medo-Persian Empire (*ibid.*, p. 116).
Copper belly and thighs: The Greek Empire (*ibid.*, p. 122).
Iron legs: The Roman Empire, later the British Empire, and finally the dual Anglo-American world power (*ibid.*, p.123).
Ten toes: Independent powers and governments vying with one another for supremacy during the time of the end (*ibid.*, p.124).
Iron and clay feet: The weakening of absolute power of governments by the spread of socialist and democratic elements (*ibid.*, p. 125).

Daniel 7 – Four Beasts:
Lion with eagle's wings: Same as the golden head – Babylonian Empire (*ibid.*, p. 170).
Bear: Same as the silver breast and arms – the Medo-Persian Empire (*ibid.*, p. 171).
Four-headed, winged leopard:
Same as the copper belly and thighs – the Greek Empire (*ibid.*, p. 172).
Ten-horned beast: Same as the iron legs – the Roman and British Empires and, finally the dual Anglo-American world power (*ibid.*, p. 174).
Little horn: The dual Anglo-American world power (*ibid.*, p. 178).

Daniel 8:3 – Ram:
Same as the bear and the silver breast and arms – Medo-Persian Empire (*ibid.*, p. 190).

Daniel 8:5 – Goat:
Same as the four-headed, winged leopard and the copper belly and thighs – the Greek Empire (*ibid.*, p. 194).

Daniel 8:13 – Transgression of desolation:
The failure, in 1926, of world governments to heed Watch Tower President Rutherford's call for them to withdraw support from the League of Nations (*ibid.*, p. 214).

Daniel 11 – King of the north:
The political power controlling the territories to the north of Jerusalem – during the time of the end this has been, first, the German Reich and then Soviet Communism (*ibid.*, pp. 278ff).

Daniel 11 – King of the south:
The political power controlling the territories to the south of Jerusalem – during the time of the end this has been, first, the British Empire and later the Anglo-American dual world power (*ibid.*, pp. 271ff).

Daniel 12:1 – Michael:
Jesus Christ, enthroned in heaven (*ibid.*, p. 312).

Daniel 12:11 – Abomination of desolation:
The League of Nations and its successor, the United Nations Organisation, especially insofar as the League was described by the Federal Council of Churches of Christ in America as 'the political expression of the Kingdom of God on earth' (*ibid.*, pp. 206ff).

Matthew 24:45 – Faithful and discreet slave:
Collectively, all those who, at any one time, belong to the 'little flock' or the 144,000 joint heirs with Christ *(God's Kingdom of a Thousand Years Has Approached*, pp. 241ff).

Matthew 24:48 – Evil slave:
Generally, all those professed Christians who, following the end of World War I, failed to take their stand for the newly inaugurated kingdom of God. Especially, those Bible Students who seceded from the Watch Tower Society during the early years of Rutherford's presidency and formed groups remaining loyal to Russell's ideas (*ibid.*, pp. 250ff).

2 Thessalonians 2:3 - Man of lawlessness:
The clergy of Christendom (*ibid.*, pp. 374ff).

Revelation 7:4 – 144,000:
Same as the 'little flock' or the true Israel of God, whose members have been selected from Pentecost AD 33 until 1935 when the 'great crowd' began to be gathered. These are the ones who are to rule with Christ in heaven. The number is regarded as literal (*Revelation – Its Grand Climax at Hand*, p. 117).

Revelation 7:9 – Great Crowd:
The unlimited number of people who have joined the Witnesses, especially since 1935, and whose eventual reward will be everlasting life on earth (*ibid.*, p. 122).

Revelation 12:1 – Woman:
The Jerusalem above, that is, Jehovah's universal organisation of spirit creatures (*ibid.*, p. 178).

Revelation 12:3 – Seven-headed, ten-horned dragon:
Satan the devil (*ibid.*, p. 178).

Revelation 12:5 – Child:
The Kingdom of God which was 'born' in heaven in 1914 (*ibid.*, p. 180).

Revelation 12:7 – Michael:
Jesus Christ, enthroned in heaven, who is the only one given the title 'archangel' (*ibid.*, p. 181).

Revelation 13:1, 2 – Seven-headed, ten-horned beast:
Satan's entire political system. The ten horns represent the totality of sovereign states, indicating that all governments throughout the world belong to this beast. The seven heads represent the succession of seven dominant world powers (*ibid.*, pp. 188f).

Revelation 13:11 – Two-horned beast from the earth:
The two horns represent the partnership of two political powers, namely, Britain and the USA referred to in Watch Tower literature as the Anglo-American world power (*ibid.*, pp. 193f).

Revelation 13:14 – Image of the beast:
The League of Nations and the United Nations (*ibid.*, p. 195).

Revelation 14:8 – Babylon the Great:
Satan's world empire of false religion which comprises all religious organisations other than the Watch Tower movement (*ibid.*, p. 205).

Revelation 16:13 – False prophet:
Same as the two-horned beast, namely, the Anglo-American world power (*ibid.*, p. 230).

Revelation 21:2 – New Jerusalem:
The bride of Christ, namely, the 144,000 enthroned with Christ. Not to be confused with the Jerusalem above (*ibid.*, p. 301).

Appendix Three
The Seven Trumpets

The seven trumpets (Rev 8:7 - 9:13; 11:16) are proclamations of Jehovah's judgement which, though continuing to characterise the Witnesses' message, are especially associated with a series of Watch Tower conventions beginning in 1922.

September 1922
Cedar Point, Ohio. First trumpet (Rev 8:7) begins to sound. World leaders challenged to account for their failure to bring peace and prosperity (*Revelation – Its Grand Climax at Hand*, p. 134).

August 1923
Los Angeles, California. Second trumpet (Rev 8:8) begins to sound. All who love peace called upon to withdraw from their churches (*ibid.*, p. 135).

July 1924
Columbus, Ohio. Third trumpet (Rev 8:10) begins to sound. Christendom's clergy indicted for their refusal to preach the kingdom of God (*ibid.*, p. 138).

August 1925
Indianapolis, Indiana. Fourth trumpet (Rev 8:12) begins to sound. God's kingdom proclaimed as the only hope for peace (*ibid.*, p. 140).

May 1926
London, England. Fifth trumpet (Rev 9:1) begins to sound. Christendom exposed as deserving God's adverse judgement for its rejection of the kingdom (*ibid.*, p. 147).

July 1927
Toronto, Canada. Sixth trumpet (Rev 9:13) begins to sound. All in Christendom called upon to abandon their churches (*ibid.*, p. 149).

July 1928
Detroit, Michigan. Seventh trumpet (Rev 11:16) begins to sound. Announcement given of the coming destruction of Satan and his evil organisation at the battle of Armageddon (*ibid.*, p. 172).

Appendix Four
The Seven Plagues

The seven plagues are 'scathing judgement pronouncements publicizing Jehovah's view of various features of this world and warning of the final outcome of his judicial decisions'. Together with the trumpets, they comprise the Witnesses' message for the world at large (*Revelation – Its Grand Climax at Hand*, p. 216).

The first plague (Rev 16:2) is directed against 'the earth' which represents the world's political systems (*ibid.*, p. 221).

The second plague (Rev 16:3) is directed against 'the sea' which represents the mass of humanity which is alienated from Jehovah (*ibid.*, p. 223).

The third plague (Rev 16:4) is directed against 'the rivers and fountains' which represents all of the world's supposed sources of wisdom and guidance (*ibid.*, p. 224).

The fourth plague (Rev 16:8) is directed against 'the sun' which represents the world's rulers (*ibid.*, p. 226).

The fifth plague (Rev 16:10) is directed against the 'throne of the wild beast' and exposes the true source of authority, namely, Satan, of the world's political systems (*ibid.*, p. 227).

The sixth plague (Rev 16:12) is directed against 'the River Euphrates' which, being dried up, results in the weakening of the defences of Babylon the Great, or false religion (*ibid.*, p. 230).

The seventh plague (Rev 16:17) is directed against 'the air' which represents 'the spirit, or general mental inclination, that characterises [Satan's] whole wicked system of things, the satanic thinking that permeates every aspect of life outside Jehovah's organization' (*ibid.*, p. 234).

Appendix Five
Continuing Bible Students

There were several groups of Bible Students who defected from the Society following the death of Russell. Of those whom Rutherford expelled whilst establishing his position as Russell's successor, and those sympathetic to them, some formed the Pastoral Bible Institute which publishes the monthly magazine, *The Herald of Christ's Kingdom*. A group known as the Standfasts was formed in 1918 objecting to a call from Watch Tower leaders for Bible Students to join in a national day of prayer for an Allied victory over Germany. Paul S. L. Johnson, who had considered himself to be the rightful successor to Russell, founded the Laymen's Home Missionary Movement around 1920. The main group of those who defected in the late 1920s and 1930s formed the Dawn Bible Students Association which publishes a monthly magazine, *The Dawn, a Herald of Christ's Presence*. Both the Dawn and the Laymen's Home Missionary Movement publish editions of Russell's *Studies in the Scriptures*.

Of all the groups of continuing Bible Students, the Laymen's Home Missionary Movement has remained closest to the teachings of Russell and tends to keep somewhat aloof from other groups which exhibit considerable variation in their beliefs about the Second Presence and the kingdom.

All the groups have dwindled but this gives no cause for concern even when compared with the massive expansion of the Witnesses. The Bible Students, regarding themselves as members of the 'little flock' and generally holding to Russell's belief about the 'great multitude' as a group that will come to prominence only after Armageddon, expect that their numbers will dwindle.

From time to time, disaffected Witnesses have joined Bible Student groups, but, although they share some significant beliefs in common, the Society's branding them as the 'evil slave' (Matthew 25:26) has fostered attitudes which make it difficult for many former Witnesses to regard them at all favourably.

Bibliography

1.   Primary Watch Tower Sources

The books and periodicals listed in this section were all published in Brooklyn USA, by the Watch Tower Bible and Tract Society, except as indicated below. This section is not an exhaustive list of Watch Tower literature, but includes only those titles that are most directly relevant to the present topic.

Russell, Charles Taze, *Tabernacle Shadows of the Better Sacrifices*, 1881.
Studies in the Scriptures, 6 vols, 1886-1904.
    Vol. 1. *The Divine Plan of the Ages*, 1886.
    Vol. 2. *The Time is at Hand*, 1889.
    Vol. 3. *Thy Kingdom Come*, 1891.
    Vol. 4. *The Battle of Armageddon*, 1897.
    Vol. 5. *The Atonement between God and Man*, 1899.
    Vol. 6. *The New Creation*, 1904.
Woodworth, Clayton J., *Bible Students' Manual*, no date or publisher given.
Fisher, George and Woodworth, Clayton J. (eds), *The Finished Mystery*, 1917.
Rutherford, Joseph Franklin, *Millions Now Living Will Never Die*, 1920.
                               The Harp of God, 1921.
                               Life, 1929.
                               Prophecy, 1929.
                               Light, 2 vols, 1930.
                               Vindication, 3 vols, 1931 and 1932.
                               Riches, 1936.
                               Enemies, 1937.

The titles below, following the Society's policy since 1942, were all published anonymously. However, the authorship, where known, is indicated in brackets.
    The New World, 1942 (Fred Franz).
    The Truth Shall Make You Free, 1943 (Fred Franz).
    The Kingdom is at Hand, 1944 (Fred Franz).
    Let God be True, 1946, revised 1952 (Fred Franz).
    This Means Everlasting Life, 1950 (Fred Franz).
    New Heavens and a New Earth, 1953 (Fred Franz).
    You May Survive Armageddon, 1955 (Fred Franz).
    Your Will be Done on Earth, 1958 (Fred Franz).
    Jehovah's Witnesses in the Divine Purpose, 1958 (Harry Peloyan).

From Paradise Lost to Paradise Restored, 1958 (Harry Peloyan).
The Word – Who is He? According to John, 1962 (Fred Franz).
Babylon the Great has Fallen, 1963 (Fred Franz).
Things in Which it is Impossible for God to Lie, 1965 (Fred Franz)
Life Everlasting in Freedom of the Sons of God, 1966 (Fred Franz).
The Truth that Leads to Eternal Life, 1968 (Fred Franz).
Then is Finished the Mystery of God, 1969 (Fred Franz).
The Nations Shall Know that I am Jehovah – How?, 1971 (Fred Franz).
Paradise Restored by Theocracy, 1972 (Fred Franz).
God's Kingdom of a Thousand Years has Approached, 1973 (Fred Franz).
True Peace and Security – From what Source?, 1973 (Harry Peloyan).
God's Eternal Purpose Now Triumphing for Man's Good, 1974 (Fred Franz).
Is This Life All There Is?, 1974 (Edward Dunlap).
Man's Salvation out of World Distress at Hand, 1975 (Fred Franz).
Good News – To Make You Happy, 1976 (Lloyd Barry).
Holy Spirit – The Force Behind the Coming New Order, 1976 (Fred Franz).
Let Your Kingdom Come, 1981.
You can Live Forever in Paradise on Earth, 1982.
The Divine Name that will Endure Forever, 1984.
Survival into a New Earth, 1984.
Life – How did it Get Here?, 1985.
Peace and Security, 1986.
Yearbook of Jehovah's Witnesses, 1987.
Revelation – Its Grand Climax at Hand, 1988.
Jehovah's Witnesses, Proclaimers of God's Kingdom, 1993.

Periodicals
The Watchtower, Announcing Jehovah's Kingdom,1939, continuing.
Awake!, 1946, continuing.

2. Secondary Sources and Other Works

Anonymous, *Behold Your King*, E. Rutherford: Dawn Bible Students Association, n.d.
The Creator's Grand Design, E. Rutherford: Dawn Bible Students Association, n.d.
Anderson, Sir Robert M., *The Coming Prince: The Marvellous Prophecy of Daniel's Seventy Weeks Concerning the Antichrist*, Grand Rapids: Kregel, 16th edition, 1967.
Bebbington, David W., *Evangelicalism in Modern Britain: A History from the 1730s to the 1970s*, London: Unwin Hyman, 1989.
Beckford, James A., *The Trumpet of Prophecy: A Sociological Analysis of Jehovah's Witnesses*, Oxford: Blackwell, 1975.
Berry, Harold J., *The Truth Twisters*, Lincoln, Nebraska: Back to the Bible, 1987.
Botting, Heather and Gary, *The Orwellian World of Jehovah's Witnesses*, Toronto: University of Toronto Press, 1984.
Cole, Marley, *Jehovah's Witnesses – The New World Society*, New York: Vantage Press, 1955.
Court, John M., *Myth and History in the Book of Revelation*, London: John Knox Press, 1979.
Damsteegt, P. Gerard, *Foundations of the Seventh Day Adventist Message and Mission*,

Grand Rapids: Eerdmans, 1977.

Franz, Raymond, *Crisis of Conscience*, Atlanta: Commentary Press, 1983. *In Search of Christian Freedom*, Atlanta: Commentary Press, 1991.

Froom, Le Roy Edwin, *The Prophetic Faith of Our Fathers*, 4 volumes, Washington: Review and Herald, 1950-54.

Gilley, Sheridan W., 'Newman and Prophecy', *The Journal of the URC History Society*, 1985.

Glasson, Thomas F., *The Second Advent: The Origin of the New Testament Doctrine*, London: Epworth, 1945. *Jesus and the End of the World*, Edinburgh: St Andrews, 1980.

Gray, James M., *Commentary on the Whole Bible*, New Jersey: Spire Books, 1971.

Gruss, Edmond C., *The Jehovah's Witnesses and Prophetic Speculation*, New Jersey: Presbyterian and Reformed Publishing Co., 2nd edition, 1975.

Harris, Doug, *Awake to the Watch Tower*, Twickenham: Reachout Trust, 1988.

Harrison, Barbara G., *Visions of Glory*, New York: Simon and Schuster, 1978.

Harrison, J. F. C., *The Second Coming: Popular Millennarianism 1780–1850*, London: Routledge & Kegan Paul, 1979.

Hartman, Louis F. and Di Lella, Alexander A., 'Daniel' in Raymond Brown *et al* (eds), *The New Jerome Biblical Commentary*, London: Geoffrey Chapman, 1991 edition.

Hilton, Boyd, *The Age of Atonement: The Influence of Evangelicalism on Social and Economic Thought 1785–1865*, Oxford: Clarendon Press, 1988.

Hoekema, Anthony A., *Jehovah's Witnesses*, Grand Rapids: Eerdmans,1973.

Hudson, Albert O., *Bible Students in Britain: The Story of a Hundred Years*, London: Bible Fellowship Union, 1989.

Hudson, W.S., *Religion in America: An Historical Account of the Development of American Religious Life*, New York: Charles Scribner's Sons, 2nd edition, 1973.

Jones, Leslie W. (ed.), *What Pastor Russell Said*, Chicago: The Bible Students Bookstore, 1917.

Jonsson, Carl O., *The Gentile Times Reconsidered*, Lethbridge: Hart, 1983.

Kellett, Arnold, *Isms and Ologies: A Guide to Unorthodox and Non-Christian Beliefs*, London: Epworth Press, 1965.

Knibb, M. A., 'Prophecy and the Emergence of Jewish Apocalypses', in Coggins, R., Phillips, A., and Knibb, M. A.(eds), *Israel's Prophetic Tradition*, Cambridge University Press, 1982.

Lacocque, Andre, *The Book of Daniel*, London: SPCK, 1979.

Ladd, George E., *The Blessed Hope: A Biblical Study of the Second Advent and the Rapture*,Grand Rapids: Eerdmans, 1956.

Lane, S. H., *Our Paradise Home*,Watford: International Tract Society, 1903.

Macmillan, Alexander H., *Faith on the March*, Englewood Cliffs: Prentice Hall, 1957.

Marsden, George M., *Fundamentalism and American Culture: The Shaping of Twentieth Century Evangelicalism, 1870-1925*, New York: Oxford University Press, 1980.

Martin, Walter and Klann, Norman, *Jehovah of the Watchtower*, Minneapolis: Bethany House, 1953, revised 1974.

Mason, Douglas, *Witnessing the Name*, Victoria, Australia: On The Watch, 2nd edition, 1985.

Miller, William, *Evidences from Scripture and History of the Second Coming of Christ, about the Year 1843*, Boston: Joshua V. Himes, 1842.

Oliver, W. H., *Prophets and Millennialists: The Uses of Biblical Prophecy in England from the 1790s to the 1840s*, Auckland, N.Z.: Auckland University Press, 1978.

Penton, M. James, *Apocalypse Delayed: The Story of Jehovah's Witnesses*, University of Toronto Press, 1985.

Porteous, Norman, *Daniel, A Commentary*, London: SCM, 1965.

Robinson, John A. T., *Jesus and His Coming: The Emergence of a Doctrine*, London: SCM, 1957.

Rogerson, Alan, *Millions Now Living Will Never Die*, London: Constable, 1969.

Ross, J. J., *Some Facts About the Self-styled Pastor, Charles T. Russell*, New York: Charles C. Cook, n.d.

Some Facts and More Facts About the Self-styled Pastor, Charles T. Russell, New York: Charles C. Cook, n.d.

Rowland, Christopher, *The Open Heaven: A Study of Apocalyptic in Judaism and Early Christianity*, London: SPCK, 1982.

Russell, D. S., *Apocalyptic: Ancient and Modern*. London: SCM, 1978.

Sandeen, Ernest R., *The Roots of Fundamentalism: British and American Millenarianism, 1800-1930*, Chicago and London: University of Chicago Press, 1970.

Schnell, William J., *Thirty Years a Watch Tower Slave*, Grand Rapids: Baker, 1956.

Smith, Uriah, *Daniel and the Revelation: The Response of History to the Voice of Prophecy*, Watford: Stanborough Press, n.d.

Spicer, W.A., *Our Day in the Light of Prophecy*, Watford: Stanborough Press, n.d.

Stevenson, William, *Year of Doom, 1975*, London: Hutchinson, 1967.

Stroup, Herbert H., *The Jehovah's Witnesses*, New York: Columbia University Press, 1945.

Thomas, John, *Elpis Israel; An Exposition of the Kingdom of God*, Birmingham: Christadelphian, 1942 edition.

von Rad, Gerhard, *Old Testament Theology*, 2 vols, London: SCM, 1975.

Weber, Timothy P., *Living in the Shadow of the Second Coming: American Premillennialism 1875-1925*, Oxford and New York: Oxford University Press, 1979.

Wenham, David, 'The Kingdom of God and Daniel', in *Expository Times*, Vol. 98, No. 5, February 1987.

Whiston, William (translator), *The Works of Flavius Josephus*, London and Edinburgh: Nimmo, n.d.

White, Timothy, *A People for His Name: A History of Jehovah's Witnesses and an Evaluation*, New York: Vantage Press, 1968.

Wilson, Benjamin, *The Emphatic Diaglott*, Brooklyn: Watch Tower Bible and Tract Society, 1902.

Wilson, Bryan, *Sects and Society*, London: Heinemann, 1961.

Index

Scripture Index

UNIVERSITY OF WOLVERHAMPTON
LEARNING RESOURCES